Tools of the Mind

The Vygotskian Approach to Early Childhood Education

Elena Bodrova and Deborah J. Leong
Metropolitan State College-Denver

Merrill,
an imprint of Prentice Hall
Englewood Cliffs, New Jersey   Columbus, Ohio

Library of Congress Cataloging-in-Publication Data
Bodrova, Elena
   Tools of the mind : the Vygotskian approach to early childhood
education / Elena Bodrova, Deborah J. Leong. — 1st ed.
      p.   cm.
   Includes bibliographical references (p.) and index.
   ISBN 0-02-369874-8 (alk. paper)
   1. Early childhood education—Philosophy. 2. Child development.
3. Constructivism (Education) 4.   Learning, Psychology of. 5. Play.
6. Early childhood education—Activity programs. 7. Vygotskiĭ, L.
S. (Lev Semenovich), 1896-1934. I. Leong, Deborah J. II. Title.
LB1139.23.L46 1996
372.21—dc20

95-20284
CIP

Cover photo: Ginni Kinder
Editor: Ann Castel Davis
Production Editor: Alexandrina Benedicto Wolf
Design Coordinator: Julia Zonneveld Van Hook
Cover Designer: Scott Rattray
Production Manager: Laura Messerly

This book was set in New Baskerville by Carlisle Communications, Ltd. and was printed and bound by Quebecor Printing/Book Press. The cover was printed by Phoenix Color Corp.

© 1996 by Prentice-Hall, Inc.
A Simon & Schuster Company
Englewood Cliffs, New Jersey 07632

Photo credits: All photos by Ginni Kinder

Printed in the United States of America

10 9 8 7 6 5 4 3 2 1

ISBN: 0-02-369874-8

Prentice-Hall International (UK) Limited, *London*
Prentice-Hall of Australia Pty. Limited, *Sydney*
Prentice-Hall of Canada, Inc., *Toronto*
Prentice-Hall Hispanoamericana, S. A., *Mexico*
Prentice-Hall of India Private Limited, *New Delhi*
Prentice-Hall of Japan, Inc., *Tokoyo*
Simon & Schuster Asia Pte. Ltd., *Singapore*
Editora Prentice-Hall do Brasil, Ltda., *Rio de Janeiro*

This book is lovingly dedicated to our families:

Dmitri and Andrei Semenov

Robert and Jeremy Leitz

Preface

We chose the title for this book, *Tools of the Mind,* because the purpose of this book is to enable teachers to arm young children with the mental tools necessary for learning, and also because the book itself is a tool for the teacher. Mental tools are ideas that we learn from others, modify, and then pass on. Vygotsky, his students, and colleagues have given us wonderful mental tools which we in turn hope to pass on to the readers of this book. This book and its related video, *Introduction to Vygotsky** by Davidson Films (1994), will give teachers a strong foundation on Vygotsky's ideas.

We have visualized the organization of the book as a set of concentric circles or a spiral, in that the content becomes more and more tightly focused as the book progresses. Section I (Chapters 1 through 3) introduces the major ideas in the Vygotskian approach and compares and contrasts this view to perspectives that will be familiar to early childhood teachers and psychology students. Section II of the book (Chapters 4, 5, and 6) revisits the points made in the first section and applies these to the learning/teaching process. Section II describes general strategies for approaching learning/teaching. Section III (Chapters 7, 8, and 9) and Section IV (Chapters 10 and 11) are even more detailed with specific applications provided. The ideas in Sections I and II are revisited again, but now in terms of actual classroom practices. Section III deals with tactics or ways of interacting with children. These tactics may be implemented in classrooms at many grade levels. Section IV focuses on applications specific to early childhood classrooms.

Examples and activities in this book are a product of a three-year collaboration with preschool, kindergarten, and first- and second-grade teachers in the Denver

---

*For further information, contact Davidson Films, Inc., 231 E. Street, Davis, CA 95616. Phone: (916) 753-9604. FAX (916) 753-3719.

metropolitan area. The programs ranged from Head Start to the Denver Public Schools to Colorado Academy, a private college-preparatory school. The classrooms ranged from traditional to multiage groups (combining kindergarten, first grade, and second grade) and were philosophically diverse, including, for example, traditional ways of teaching reading as well as whole language. Some of the classrooms had bilingual instruction. The demographic makeup of the classrooms was also diverse, ranging from classes with large proportions of at-risk and homeless children to classes with mostly privileged children at a private school.

One of the most exciting things we have found in our work with teachers is that the Vygostskian approach works in all of the classrooms we have described. Many of the concerns addressed in this book go beyond socioeconomic class or classroom philosophy. Vygotsky helps us examine our roles as the adults in the classroom in a different way, providing many more alternatives for action.* He helps us see ourselves as partners with children in the great journey to learn, rather than as task masters or followers. Our work with teachers and children in these various classrooms has been a liberating, exhilarating, and exciting endeavor, reminding many of us of why we became teachers in the first place!

Throughout the book we have balanced the examples by using children of different ages, so that all of the early childhood period is presented. Because English lacks a gender-neutral pronoun for *child* and *teacher,* we alternate between using *he* and *she.*

Acknowledgments

We have many people to thank for their contributions to this book. First we want to thank the many teachers, children, and parents at Colorado Academy, Metropolitan State College, Head Start, Child Development Center (Denver), the Early Education Collaboration Project of the Denver Public Schools, and Crofton-Ebert Elementary School. Many of the teachers critiqued the manuscript for the book, tried out activities, and documented what happened when they did them. In particular, we want to thank Paula Osborne, Carol Lanaghen, and Carriellen De Muth, the first teachers with whom we worked, whose enthusiasm and ability to translate theory into practice astounded us. In addition, we want to thank Donna Brady-Lawler, Ricki Feist, Nicole Walravens, Pat Duran, Irene Ribera, Gloria Ky, Richard Raynor, Kathy Snow, Sandy Green, Ruth Hensen, Christy Crane, and Margaret Wachtler for their willingness to try activities out in their classrooms and for their feedback on several chapters of the book. Also, thanks to Laura Brophy, Debra Pritchard, Deborah Ross, David Cornwell, Lynn Trow-Hammond, and Julie Holscher for their participation in our work. Our special thanks to the gifted administrators from these programs who read chapters and gave us more than just administrative support: Dr. Tom Fitzgerald, Paula Biewer, Mary Ann Bash, Kim Deitsch, and Judith Crider. In addition, we would like to recognize Dr. Rex Brown, Chris Babbs, Mary Curtis, Suzanne Adams, and Marge Petersen for their assistance. We would also like to express our appreciation to our research assistants, who helped us collect data and reviewed chapters: Lorraine Burns, Lori Smith, Joan Taylor, Jerry Eurich, Lisa Rimmer, Leah Schneider, Jennifer Lawrence, Carolyn Erhart, Jenny Jenkins, and Renea Gomez.

Much of our work in the schools would not have been possible without the efforts of Carolyn Schaeffer, Brenda Byrne, and Steven Moss, whose grant-writing skills enabled us to obtain the financial support to try out ideas in the classroom. The following foundations provided generous support: Kraft Foods, Security Life (ING) Group of Denver, Martin Marietta, Astronautics, and ARCO, Eduquest/IBM, Hewlett-Packard, and the William & Mary Griere Foundation, Inc.

The following colleagues gave us moral support and critiqued the manuscript: Lyn Wickelgren, Fran Davidson (Davidson Films), and Joan Foster. Thanks also to Alan Dahms, David Day, Carol Nichols, and Lois Holzman. A special thanks to Oralie McAfee, who acted as our mentor and friend throughout this process.

We would like to thank the Denver public school administration for their leadership. Special thanks goes to Turila Norman and Irv Moskowitz.

We would also like to thank the following reviewers for their invaluable feedback: Jerold P. Bauch, Vanderbilt University; Cary Buzzelli, Indiana University; Marjorie V. Fields, University of Alaska, S.E.; Joanne Hendrick, University of Oklahoma; Alice S. Honig, Syracuse University; James E. Johnson, The Pennsylvania State University; Florence Leonard, Towson State University; Sally Lubeck, The University of Michigan; Karen Menke Paciorele, Eastern Michigan University; Carol Seefeldt, University of Maryland; C. Stephen While, University of Georgia; and Sue C. Wortham, The University of Texas at San Antonio.

Contents

The Vygotskian Framework: The Cultural-Historical Theory of Development

This section introduces the major principles in the Cultural-Historical Theory of development proposed by L. S. Vygotsky and implemented by scholars in Russia and the United States. In addition, it compares Vygotsky's perspective with other theories of child development. There are three chapters in this section:

Chapter 1   Introduction to the Vygotskian Approach

Chapter 2   Acquiring Mental Tools and Higher Mental Functions

Chapter 3   The Vygotskian Framework and Other Theories of Child Development

Introduction to the Vygotskian Approach

Tannette, who is four years old, is playing Simon Says with her friends. She keeps doing things when Simon doesn't say, as well as when he does. When she repeats aloud to herself "Simon says," she is able to stay in the game and only mimic at the right time.

Six-year-old Juan is listening to a story read by the teacher. He knows Mr. Swanson is going to ask someone in the group to retell the story. He concentrates hard and draws a picture as he listens. Later, this picture helps him to remember the story.

Maura, a sixth grader, is a thoughtful, deliberate problem solver. When she has to answer a question, her answers seem intentional, and she thinks before she speaks. She ponders complex problems, planning her approach before she begins and looking over her work.

What do these three children have in common? Each is using "tools of the mind" to help them solve problems and to remember. The idea of tools of the mind was developed by Lev Vygotsky, a Russian psychologist (1896–1934), to explain how children acquire increasingly advanced mental abilities.

Tools of the Mind

A tool is something that helps us solve problems, an instrument that facilitates performing an action. A lever helps us lift a rock that is too heavy to move with only our arms. A saw helps us cut wood that we cannot break with our hands. These physical tools extend our abilities, enabling us to do things beyond our natural capacities.

Just as we humans have invented physical tools, like hammers and forklifts, to increase our physical capacities, we have also created mental tools, or *tools of the mind,* to extend our mental abilities. These mental tools help us to attend, remember, and think better. For example, mental tools, such as memory strategies, enable us to double and triple the amount of information we recall. Mental tools, however, do more than extend our natural abilities. Vygotsky believed they actually change the very way we attend, remember, and think.

Because they believe that mental tools play a critical role in the development of the mind, Vygotskians have explored ways in which children acquire these tools. They suggest that the role of the teacher is to "arm children" with these tools. This sounds simple, but the process involves more than merely direct teaching. It involves enabling the child to use the tool independently and creatively. As children grow and develop, they become active tool users and tool makers; they become crafters. Eventually, they will be able to use mental tools appropriately and invent new tools when necessary (Paris & Winograd, 1990). The teacher's role is to provide the path to independence—a goal of all educators.

Why Mental Tools Are Important

When children lack mental tools, they don't know how to learn. They are unable to focus the mind deliberately. As we will see, children develop the ability to use different mental tools at different ages. Their "tool chests" aren't filled all at once but gradually. Here are some examples of children who do not have mental tools.

Four-year-old Amanda is sitting in group time when the teacher asks the children to hold up their hand if they are wearing yellow. Amanda looks down at her dress and sees a gigantic brown kitty. She forgets all about "yellow," but she still holds up her hand.

Jane, who is five, knows that she is supposed to hold up her hand when another child is talking and wait until the teacher calls on her. However, she can't seem to stop herself from talking out of turn. When you ask her, she can tell you the rule. In fact, she is always telling other children the rule, even as she is blurting out answers herself.

Second grader Ben is working on his journal in a small group. He gets up to sharpen his pencil, but as he walks past the book section, he stops and looks at a book. Soon another book catches his eye. When it is time to change activities, he notices he is still holding a dull pencil, and he no longer has any time left to complete his work.

Eight-year-old Tony is solving a word problem: There are some birds sitting on a tree. Three flew away and seven are left. How many birds were there in the tree in the beginning? Tony keeps subtracting 3 from 7. Instead of adding, he subtracts because of the word "away". He doesn't self-regulate or check his thinking. Even though his teacher has just explained that estimating will help, he doesn't apply the strategy to this problem.

Young children *are* able to think, attend, and remember. The problem is that their thinking, attention, and memory are very reactive; the object or activity must hold their attention. Think about how children learn so many things by watching television, especially commercials. Very simply, television exploits reactive thinking, memory, and attention. Television is loud, has lots of movement, changes scenes every few seconds, and is colorful. This format is used to teach basic skills in programs like Sesame Street, but many teachers complain that the fast-paced sensory bombardment tends to make it difficult to teach some children in other ways. In fact, many early childhood teachers complain that they have to "sing, dance, or act like Big Bird" in order to teach. Without the acquisition of mental tools, this attention-grabbing approach would be the only way for children to acquire information, because children could not direct and focus their attention, memory, and problem-solving skills on their own.

When children have mental tools, they can take more responsibility for learning on their own because learning becomes a self-directed activity. The teacher no longer has to take total responsibility for every aspect of the learning process. Tools relieve teachers of this unnecessary burden, and more important, they can be applied across the curriculum, from reading to math or manipulatives to dramatic play.

One of the great strengths of the Vygotskian approach is that the mechanisms for teaching mental tools have been tried and tested. Instead of just expecting the tools to be learned and leaving children to struggle on their own, Vygotsky shows us ways to facilitate acquisition. Teachers in the United States and Russia who use these techniques report that they can see changes in the way that children think and learn (e.g., Palincsar, Brown, & Campione, 1993; Davydov, 1969/1991).

The absence of mental tools has long-term consequences for learning because they influence the level of abstract thinking a child can attain. To understand abstract concepts in science and math, children must have mental tools. Without them children can recite many scientific facts, but they cannot apply the facts to abstract problems or problems that are slightly different from the ones presented in the original learning situation. Vygotsky traces this lack of transfer from one setting to the next to an absence of mental tools. While abstract problems are the concern of teachers in the upper elementary grades, the tools learned during the early childhood period have a direct bearing on later abilities.

Logical, abstract thought is needed not just in school but in making informed decisions in many areas of adult life. How to buy a car, manage one's finances, decide how to vote, participate in a jury, and raise children all require mature thinking skills.

History of the Vygotskian Approach

The Life of Vygotsky

The Russian psychologist Lev Vygotsky lived from 1896 to 1934 and produced over 180 articles, books, and research studies. Vygotsky also suffered from tuberculosis from a young age and the disease eventually killed him at the age of 38. Throughout his whole life he triumphed over difficulties. He faced difficulty getting an education. Born in Gomel, Vygotsky was a Jew. In prerevolutionary Russia strict limits were set on the number of Jews that could be educated at the university level, but Vygotsky won a place and became an exceptional student. As a psychologist, Vygotsky faced intense pressure to modify his theory to fit the prevailing political dogma. He did not succumb to the pressure. Several years after his death, however, his ideas were repudiated and expunged. The problem of political correctness also affected the work of his students, who courageously continued to expand and elaborate on his theory in spite of the risks. We have these scholars to thank for keeping Vygotsky's ideas alive. When the intellectual thaw of the late fifties and early sixties occurred, these scholars revived Vygotsky's ideas, applying them in many areas of education.

Vygotsky's interests ranged from cognitive and language development to literary analysis to special education. He taught literature in a secondary school and then went on to lecture at a teacher-training institute. He became very interested in psychology and gave a presentation in Leningrad (St. Petersburg) on consciousness that brought him much acclaim. After moving his family to Moscow, he began a collaboration with Alexander Luria and Alexei Leont'ev that resulted in the rich theory and body of research that we have come to know as the Vygotskian approach.

Lev Vygotsky

If you are interested in learning more about Vygotsky and his colleagues and students, Van der Veer and Valsiner (1991) and Kozulin (1990) give a detailed account of the life of Vygotsky and his ideas both in and outside of Russia. In addition, Alexander Luria's autobiography (1979) makes fascinating reading.

Vygotsky's theory of development was unique and distinct from those of his contemporaries and is often called the *Cultural-Historical Theory*. Because his life was so short, his theory leaves many unanswered questions and is not always sufficiently supported by empirical data. Over the years, however, many of his concepts have been elaborated and studied by scholars in Russia and the West. Presently, his theory is changing the way psychologists think about development and the way educators work with young children.

In a strict sense, Vygotskian theory is really a framework for understanding learning and teaching. It gives the early childhood educator a new perspective and helpful insights about children's growth and development. Although it does not define a set of premises and present empirical studies that provide recipes for any classroom situation, teachers can expect his ideas to inspire them to see children in a different way and consequently to modify the ways they interact with and teach them.

Vygotsky's Contemporaries

Among the major Western theorists in psychology that Vygotsky studied and reacted to were Piaget (constructivism), Watson and Skinner (behaviorism), Freud (psychoanalysis), and Koffka (Gestalt psychology). In his theoretical papers and empirical studies, Vygotsky proposed alternative explanations for several of Piaget's early works concerning the development of language in young children. Vygotsky also commented on the work of Montessori. For a discussion of the similarities and differences between the Vygotskian framework and other developmental psychologists, see Chapter 3.

Russian Colleagues and Students

Vygotsky collaborated with his colleagues Alexander Luria (1902–1977) and Alexei Leont'ev (1903–1979) on many of his early experiments, and they contributed to the development of the framework. After Vygotsky's death, Luria, Leont'ev, and other Vygotskians faced increased pressure to cease their research. Many of them carried on their research but did not openly acknowledge the tie to Vygotsky until the political winds changed. They elaborated on the major principles and applied them to various areas of psychology.

Luria, one of Vygotsky's most prolific colleagues, pioneered studies in such varied areas as cross-cultural psychology, neuropsychology, and psycholinguistics. He applied Vygotskian principles to the study of neuropsychology by looking at brain damage and possible ways of compensating for it. In cross-cultural psychology, Luria (1976) also studied how cultural influences shape cognition. Luria's psycholinguistic research probed the role of private speech in the regulation of motor actions and examined the ties between language and cognition from a developmental as well as clinical perspective. Vocate (1987) gives an excellent summary of Luria and his work.

Leont'ev (1977/1978) studied deliberate memory and attention and developed his own theory of activity which linked the social context or environment to developmental accomplishments through the child's own actions. Leont'ev's theory is the basis of much current research in Russia, especially in the areas of play and learning. Some of these studies and their application to early childhood development will be discussed in detail in Chapters 5 and 6.

Piotr Gal'perin (1902–1988), Daniil Elkonin (1904–1985), and Alexandr Zaporozhets (1905–1981), three of Vygotsky's students, focused on the structure and development of learning/teaching processes. Zaporozhets founded the Institute of Preschool Education where he and his students applied the Vygotskian approach to early childhood education. Today the Vygotskian tradition in educational and developmental psychology is being carried on in Russia by scholars such as Vasili Davydov (1991) and Vitali Rubtsov (1991). Their elaborations of Vygotsky's original ideas have led to many of the innovations in teaching practices discussed in this book.

Contemporary Research and Applications

Western psychologists first became interested in Vygotsky in the late 1960s following the translation of his *Thought and Language* ([1934]1962). Psychologists in

Scandinavia, Germany, and Holland have addressed broad philosophical issues in this framework. American psychologists Michael Cole and Sylvia Scribner (1973), Jerome Bruner (1985), and Uri Bronfenbrenner (1977) first brought Vygotsky to the attention of psychologists and educators in the United States. In the 1970s-1990s interest in the social-cognitive aspects of the Vygotskian framework was promoted by other researchers such as Wertsch (1991a), Rogoff (1991), Tharp and Gallimore (1988), Cazden (1993), Campione and Brown (1990), and John-Steiner (1990). At first American researchers were interested in the global aspects of Vygotsky's theory, but more recent research has been more specialized, studying how the framework applies in different areas of psychology and education. For example, several researchers have focused on a comparison of Vygotskian and non-Vygotskian approaches to play (Berk, 1994) or joint problem solving (Newman, Griffin, & Cole, 1989). The Vygotskian framework has been used in a number of programs in the United States and other countries outside of Russia. Most of the efforts have involved elementary, middle school, and high school students (Campione and Brown, 1990; Feuerstein & Feuerstein, 1991; Newman, Griffin, & Cole, 1989). However, few programs have used the Vygotskian approach with preschool and kindergarten children. The latest NAEYC publication on Vygotsky (Berk & Winsler, 1995) presents evidence of the growing popularity of Vygotsky's ideas among early childhood educators. With the inclusion of the Vygotskian approach in the revised version of *Developmentally Appropriate Practice* (Bredecamp, in press), we anticipate greater use of these ideas in early childhood education.

This book synthesizes Vygotskian works, the work of Vygotksy's colleagues, and contemporary research in Russia, the United States, and Europe to explain how the Vygotskian framework applies to the early childhood classroom. Vygotsky's ideas form a general approach that is helpful for examining developmental processes and for finding creative ways to enhance and further a child's development.

The Vygotskian Framework: Principles of Psychology and Education

The basic principles underlying the Vygotskian framework can be summarized as follows:

1. Children construct knowledge.
2. Development cannot be separated from its social context.
3. Learning can lead development.
4. Language plays a central role in mental development.

The Construction of Knowledge

Like Piaget, Vygotsky believed that children construct their own understandings and do not passively reproduce what is presented to them. However, for Piaget, cognitive construction occurs primarily in interaction with physical objects (Ginsberg & Opper, 1988). People play an indirect role, for example, in planning the environment or creating cognitive dissonance. For Vygotsky, cognitive construction is always *socially mediated;* it is influenced by present and past social interactions. The things a teacher points out to her student will influence what that student "constructs." If one teacher points out that the blocks are distinct sizes, that student will construct a different concept than the student whose teacher points out the blocks' color. The teacher's ideas mediate or influence what and how the child will learn.

Vygotsky believed that both physical manipulation and social interaction are necessary for development. Trudy must touch, physically compare, arrange and rearrange the blocks before she acquires the concept of "big and little" and incorporates it into her own cognitive repertoire. Without manipulation and hands-on experience, Trudy will not construct her own understanding. If she has only her teacher's ideas or words, chances are that Trudy will not be able to apply the concept to slightly different materials or use it when the teacher is not present. On the other hand, without her teacher the child's learning would not be the same. Through social interaction Trudy learns which characteristics are most important, what to notice and act upon. The teacher has a direct influence on Trudy's learning through shared activity.

Because of the emphasis on the construction of knowledge, the Vygotskian approach stresses the importance of identifying what the child actually understands. Through sensitive and thoughtful exchanges with the child, the teacher discovers exactly what the child's concept is. In the Vygotskian tradition, it is common to think of learning as *appropriation* of knowledge, which underscores the active role that the learner plays in this process.

The Importance of Social Context

For Vygotsky, the *social context* influences learning more than attitudes and beliefs; it has a profound influence on how and what we think. The social context molds cognitive processes, while it is also part of the developmental process. Social context means the entire social milieu, that is, everything in the child's environment that has either been directly or indirectly influenced by the culture. The social context should be considered at several levels:

1. The immediate interactive level, that is, the individual(s) the child is interacting with at the moment
2. The structural level, which includes the social structures that influence the child such as the family and school
3. The general cultural or social level, which includes features of society at large such as language, numerical systems, and the use of technology

All of these contexts influence the way a person thinks. For example, the child whose mother emphasizes learning the names of objects will think in a different way from the child whose mother issues terse commands and does not talk with her child. The first child will not only have a larger vocabulary but will also think in different categories and use language differently (Luria, 1979; Rogoff, Malkin, & Gilbride, 1984).

Social structures also influence a child's cognitive processes. Russian research-ers found that children raised in orphanages did not have the same level of plan-ning and self-regulatory skills as children raised in families (Sloutsky, 1991). American researchers found that schools, one of the many social structures out-side of the family, directly impact the cognitive processes presumed to underpin IQ (Ceci, 1991).

The general features of the society also influence the way we think. Asian chil-dren who used an abacus had different concepts of number than children who did not (D'Ailly, 1992). These examples illustrate the pervasive influence of the social context on cognition.

The characteristics of cognition: content and processes.   A number of theorists have discussed the idea that development requires the acquisition of culturally gen-erated knowledge. Vygotsky extended this idea to include both the content and form of knowledge, the very nature of the mental processes. For example, children in Papua, New Guinea will not only know different types of animals than children in the United States, but the strategies they use to remember these animals will also differ. Children who attend school and are taught scientific categories for classify-ing animals will actually group animals in a different way than children who do not attend school. Luria (1979) found that illiterate adults from a herding community in central Asia used situationally based categories, and thus placed hammer, saw, log, and hatchet in the same category because they are all needed for work. Adults with varying amounts of school experience grouped the objects into two cate-gories, tools (hammer, saw, and hatchet) and objects to be worked on (log).

The idea that culture influences cognition is crucial because the child's entire social world shapes not just what he knows but how he thinks. The kind of logic we use and the methods we use to solve problems are influenced by our cultural expe-rience. Unlike many Western theorists, Vygotsky did not believe that there are many logical processes that are universal or culture-free. A child does not just become a thinker and a problem solver; she becomes a special kind of thinker, rememberer, listener, and communicator, which is a reflection of the social context.

Social context is a historical concept. For Vygotsky, the human mind is the prod-uct of both human history or *phylogeny,* and a person's individual history, or *ontogeny.* The modern human mind has evolved with the history of the human species. Each individual's mind is also a product of unique personal experiences.

Before they began producing tools and developing a social system for coopera-tion, human beings evolved in a way similar to other animals. When humans began to use language and to develop tools, *cultural evolution* became the mechanism that shaped further development. Through culture, one generation passes knowledge and skills on to the next. Each generation adds new things, and thus the cumulative experience and information of the culture are passed on to succeeding generations. Vygotsky assumed that children do not invent all of their knowledge and under-standing but appropriate the rich body of knowledge accumulated in their culture. The developing child acquires this information and uses it in thinking. Thus the cultural history of our ancestors influences not just our knowledge but our very thought processes.

Vygotsky believed that an individual's mind is also formed by individual history. Even though there are common aspects to mental processes, a child's mind is the result of his interactions with others within a specific social context. The child's attempts to learn and society's attempts to teach through parents, teachers, and peers all contribute to the the way a child's mind works.

The development of mental processes.   Social context plays a central role in development because it is critical for the acquisition of mental processes. Vygotsky's unique contribution was to see the possibility of the sharing of higher mental processes. Mental processes not only exist internally to the individual but can occur in an exchange between several people. Children learn or acquire a mental process by *sharing*, or using it in interacting with others. Only after this period of shared experience can the child internalize and use the mental process independently.

The idea of socially shared cognition is very different from the idea of cognition commonly accepted in Western psychology. Western tradition has viewed cognition as a set of internal mental processes accessible only to the individual. However, as researchers have studied the Vygotskian framework, a growing number have begun to examine the idea of cognition as a shared process and to recognize the importance of social context in the acquisition of these mental processes (Solomon, 1994; Resnick, 1991).

To understand the idea of a shared mental process, let's look at Western and Vygotskian descriptions of how memory develops. In the Western tradition, we would attribute Ariel's ability to remember something to the fact that she possesses a set of memory strategies and encodes the information in memory. Memory is something that is internal. Because Ariel is four years old, she will probably not remember certain things because her strategies are immature. How will she acquire mature strategies? With age, her mind will mature and she will have them.

In contrast to seeing memory only as an internal process, Vygotsky believed that memory can be shared between two people. Ariel and her teacher share memory; their interaction contains the mental process of memory. For example, Ariel has forgotten the directions to playing a game. The information is stored somewhere in her memory, but she cannot retrieve it by herself. Her teacher, on the other hand, knows some strategies for recalling the information, but he doesn't know this particular game. Thus recalling the directions of the game requires both participants. The child cannot do it alone, but the teacher cannot either. It is through their social exchange, dialogue, or interaction that they can remember. The teacher says, "What do you do with the dice?" The child says, "You throw them and they tell you how many you can move." It is in the interchange that the memory exists for now. As Ariel grows she will appropriate the strategy that she currently shares. Soon she will ask herself questions about what the rules of the game might be. At this point in her development, however, she cannot generate the questions independently.

In another example, Andre, a second grader, is trying to solve a chess problem. His father identifies the problem and suggests several alternative moves. The child chooses a move and successfully captures the pawn. The problem is solved in a shared way with both participating. Playing chess several days later, Andre uses his father's moves independently.

Thus for Vygotsky, all mental processes exist first in a shared space, and then move to an individual plane. The social context is actually part of the developmental and learning process. Shared activity is the means that facilitates a child's internalization of mental processes. Vygotsky did not deny the role of maturation, but he emphasized the importance of shared experience for cognitive development.

The Relationship of Learning and Development

Learning and development are two different processes that are complexly related to each other. Unlike behaviorists who believe that learning and development are the same thing, Vygotsky argued that there are qualitative changes in thought not accounted for only by the accumulating of facts or skills. He believed that the child's thinking gradually becomes more structured and deliberate.

While Vygotsky believed that there were maturational prerequisites for specific cognitive accomplishments, he did not believe that maturation totally determines development. Maturation influences whether the child can do certain things. For example, children could not learn logical thinking without having mastered language. However, theorists who stress maturation as the major developmental process believe that a specific level of development must exist *before* the child can learn new information. For example, Piaget's work (Inhelder & Piaget, 1958) suggests that a child must attain the stage of concrete operations before she can think logically. In this view, the internal reorganization of thinking precedes the ability to learn new things. Thus, when information is presented at a higher level, the child cannot learn it until that developmental level has been attained.

In the Vygotskian framework, not only can development impact learning, but learning can impact development. There is a complex, nonlinear relationship between learning and development. While Vygotsky did not question the existence of developmental prerequisites that limit a child's ability to learn new information at any time, he also believed that learning hastens and even causes development. For example, three-year-old Cecily is classifying objects, but she cannot keep the categories straight. Her teacher gives her two boxes, each marked with a word and a picture. One box has the word *big* in large letters with a picture of a large teddy bear. The other has the word *little* in small print with the picture of a small teddy bear. The teacher helps Cecily learn by giving her the boxes that help her keep the categories straight. Soon Cecily is categorizing other objects without the benefit of the boxes. The learning of *big* and *little* will hasten the development of categorical thinking.

Vygotsky insisted that we must consider the child's developmental level and also present information at a level that will lead the child into development. In some areas, a child must accumulate a great deal of learning before development or qualitative change occurs. In other areas, one step in learning can cause two steps in development. If we insist that development must come first, we reduce teaching to presenting material that the child already knows. Experienced teachers know that children quickly become bored when you teach a skill they already can do. But if we completely ignore the child's developmental level, we would miss the moment when children are ready to learn and consequently present material that is frustratingly difficult. An example of this type of error would be introducing addition before a child can count accurately.

Vygotsky's ideas about the relationship between learning and development are also helpful in explaining why teaching is so difficult. We cannot make exact prescriptions that produce developmental changes for every child since individual differences are to be expected. We cannot say to a teacher, "If you do this six times, every child will develop a particular skill." The exact relationship between learning and development may be different for each child and for different areas of development. Teachers must constantly adjust their methods to accommodate the learning and teaching process for each child. This is a great challenge for all educators.

The Role of Language in Development

We tend to think that language's primary impact is on the content of a person's knowledge. What we think about and what we know are influenced by the symbols and concepts that we know. Vygotsky believed that language plays a greater role in cognition. Language is an actual mechanism for thinking, a mental tool. Language makes thinking more abstract, flexible, and independent from the immediate stimuli. Through language, memories and anticipations of the future are brought to bear on the new situation, thus influencing its outcome. When children use symbols and concepts to think, they no longer need to have the object present in order to think about it. Language allows the child to imagine, manipulate, create new ideas, and share those ideas with others. It is one of the ways we exchange social information with each other. Thus language has two roles; it is instrumental in the development of cognition and is also itself part of cognitive processing.

Because learning occurs in shared situations, language is an important tool for appropriating other mental tools. To share an activity, we must talk about that activity. Unless we talk, we will never be able to know each other's meanings. Joshua and his teacher are working with Cuisenaire rods. Unless they talk about the relationships between the blocks, the teacher will not know if he has built the quantity 5 out of the units because he understands the relationship between the small rods and the larger rods. Perhaps Joshua is focusing on the color of the smaller rods and doesn't even notice that five little ones make a rod the same size as the fives rod. Only by talking can the teacher distinguish relevant from irrelevant attributes. Only by talking can Joshua make known how he understands the activity. Only by talking can Joshua and the teacher share this activity.

Language facilitates the shared experiences necessary for building cognitive processes. Six-year-old Lucy and her teacher are watching butterflies breaking out of the cocoons and drying their wings. Lucy says, "Look, they don't look bright to begin with." The teacher says, "When do they become bright? Look at that one that is just pulling itself out. Why would its wings be a different color compared to the wings of a butterfly that has been flying around for a while?" Lucy and the teacher discuss the butterflies they both see. Through many dialogues like these, Lucy will not only learn about butterflies and caterpillars, but will also acquire the cognitive processes involved in scientific discovery.

For Further Reading

Berk, L. E., & Winsler, A. (1995). Scaffolding children's learning: Vygotsky and early childhood education. *NAEYC Research and Practice Series, 7.* Washington, DC: National Association for the Education of Young Children.

Crain, W. C. (1991). *Theories of development: Concepts and applications.* Englewood Cliffs, NJ: Prentice-Hall.

Kozulin, A. (1990). *Vygotsky's psychology: A biography of ideas.* Cambridge: Cambridge University Press.

Sutherland, P. (1992). *Cognitive development today: Piaget and his critics.* London: Paul Chapman.

Van der Veer, R., & Valsiner, J. (1991) *Understanding Vygotsky: A quest for synthesis.* Cambridge: Blackwell.

Wertsch, J. V. (1991a) *Voices of the mind: A sociocultural approach to mediated action.* Cambridge: Harvard University Press.

CHAPTER 2

Acquiring Mental Tools and Higher Mental Functions

For Vygotsky, the purpose of learning, development, and teaching is more than acquiring and transmitting a body of knowledge; it involves the acquisition of tools. We teach to arm children with tools, and children appropriate these tools to master their own behavior, gain independence, and reach a higher developmental level. Vygotsky associated the higher developmental level with the use of mental tools and the emergence of higher mental functions.

The Purpose of Tools

Vygotsky believed that the difference between humans and lower animals is that humans possess tools. Humans use tools, make new tools, and teach others how to use them. These tools extend human abilities by enabling people to do things that they could not do without them. For example, although you can cut cloth to a certain extent with your teeth or hands, you can do it more easily and more precisely using scissors or knife. Physical tools enable humans to survive in and to master a changing environment.

Humans, unlike all other animals including apes, invent both physical and mental tools. The whole history of human culture can be viewed as the development of increasingly complex mental tools. Mental tools evolved from the first scratches on cave walls representing numbers to the complex categories and concepts used in modern science and mathematics. The use of the mental tools in processes such as memory and problem solving has been transmitted from generation to generation.

Extending the Mind's Capacities

Vygotsky's extension of the idea of tools to the human mind is a novel and unique way of viewing mental development. Vygotsky proposed that mental tools are to the mind as mechanical tools are to the body. Mental tools extend the mind's capacity to allow humans to adapt to their environment, and thus have a function similar to that of mechanical tools. Just like mechanical tools, mental tools can be used, invented, and taught to others.

Unlike mechanical tools, mental tools have two forms. In the early stages of development (both phylogeny *and* ontogeny), mental tools have an external, concrete, physical manifestation. At more advanced stages, these become internalized or exist in the mind without external support. An external manifestation of a mental tool is the use of a string around your finger to help you remember to buy apples at the grocery store. The internalized mental tool would be mentally associating apples with the grocery store.

Mastering Behavior

Another difference between mental and mechanical tools is their purpose. Mental tools help humans to master their own behavior, not just the environment. Without mental tools, humans would be limited to reacting to the environment as animals do. Mental tools enable humans to plan ahead, to create complex solutions to problems, and to work with others towards a common goal.

For example, the ability of humans to remember how to navigate long distances is limited in comparison to that of songbirds or other animals that use biologically programmed responses to outside stimuli, such as light patterns. Humans use mental tools to help gain control over this behavior; they might leave a pile of stones to mark the way, make a scratch on a tree, or compose a song about the landmarks along the way. Maps and compasses are physical tools that reflect advanced mental processing about the problem of navigating long distances.

Mental tools help children master their own physical, cognitive, and emotional behaviors. With mental tools, children make their bodies react in a specific pattern, for example, to music or a verbal command. Planning, problem solving, and memory are not possible without tools. Tools also help children master emotions. Instead of hitting another person when angry, they learn ways of thinking, or strategies, to control their feelings. "Counting to ten" and "thinking of something else" are tools to subdue anger.

Let's look at how mental tools, such as language, help children to control their behavior. Toddlers are not able to resist touching objects with dials and knobs because they do not have control over their impulses. In Vygotsky's words, children who lack this self-control have not yet "mastered their own behavior." When children begin to acquire this mastery, they will issue commands to themselves to help them stop doing something. Two-and-a-half-year-old Thomas says "No, don't touch" when coming near the stereo he knows he shouldn't touch. Six months earlier, Thomas did not have this tool and would run to touch the stereo. Only his mother's words and presence in front of the stereo would stop him. His actions were a reaction to the buttons and levers on the machine. When Thomas can stop himself by saying "No, don't touch," Vygotsky would say he has learned a mental tool and has become the master of his own behavior. Thomas' speech is the mental tool that enables him to regulate his actions on his own.

Gaining Independence

Vygotsky believed that when children have acquired mental tools, they will use the tools in an independent manner. Children begin by sharing the process of using the tool with others; the process is *interpersonal* at this stage. In the Vygotskian framework, the words *shared, distributed,* and *interpersonal* all stand for the idea that mental processes exist between two or more people. As children incorporate the tool into their own thought processes, a shift occurs and the tool becomes *intrapersonal, or individual.* Children no longer need to share the tool, because they can use the tool independently. Thus, gaining independence is associated with a child's moving from shared possession of tools to individual possession.

Nadia has a hard time concentrating during the morning group meeting. She lies down on other children, pokes them, and constantly talks, interrupting the teacher. The teacher has said "I like the way Mindy is paying attention" or "Pay attention" hundreds of times without the slightest impact on Nadia's behavior. The teacher realizes that Nadia does not possess the tools that will help her to concentrate on purpose. So she sits Nadia in the front of the meeting where she can put her hand on her shoulder, and she gestures to the book and says "Nadia, listen." At this point, attention still exists in a shared state, between Nadia and the teacher. After a number of group meetings, Nadia begins to concentrate on her own. Now attention is individual; Nadia is able to do it by herself.

Reaching the Highest Level of Development

The highest level of development is associated with the ability to perform and self-regulate complex cognitive operations. Children cannot reach this level through maturation or the accumulation of experiences with objects alone. The emergence of this higher level of cognitive development depends on the appropriation of tools through formal and informal instruction.

Language: The Universal Tool

Language is a universal tool that has been developed in all human cultures. It is a cultural tool because it is created and shared by all members of a specific culture. It is also a mental tool because each member of the culture uses language to think.

Language is a primary mental tool because it facilitates the acquisition of other tools and is used for many mental functions. Tools are appropriated or learned through shared experience which exists, in part, because we talk to each other. Two-year-old Frank and his teacher are putting together a puzzle. They share the experience through their physical interaction over the puzzle. However, the learning that Frank will take away from the experience depends on the language that he and his teacher share. The teacher says, "Look for a piece that has blue, because the piece next to this one is blue." Frank says, "Dis?" The teacher says, "Yes, that is blue. It matches this spot here. Keep turning it until it fits." The dialogue elevates Frank's learning to a higher level, arming him with strategies for other puzzles. Without language, Frank would not even know that there are strategies!

Language can be used to create strategies for the mastery of many mental functions, such as attention, memory, feelings, and problem solving. Saying to yourself "Only size matters" will focus your attention on the size of an object and help you ignore the other attributes. Language plays a large role in what we remember and how we remember. Because of its application to so many mental functions, we devote all of Chapter 8 to the discussion of the various aspects of language in the Vygotskian framework.

The Concept of Higher Mental Functions

Higher and Lower Mental Functions

To Vygotsky, mental processes can be divided into lower mental functions and higher mental functions. *Lower mental functions,* common to both higher animals and human beings, depend primarily on maturation to develop. Examples of lower mental functions are cognitive processes such as sensation, reactive attention, spontaneous memory, and sensorimotor intelligence. Sensation refers to using any of the five senses in mental processing. For example, pigeons can be trained to react differently to two shades of grey. Reactive attention refers to attention that is dominated by strong environmental stimuli, as when a dog suddenly attends to the sound of a car coming up the driveway. Spontaneous memory, or associative memory, is the ability to remember after two stimuli are presented together many, many times, such as associating a tune from a commercial with a company logo. Sensorimotor intelligence in the Vygotskian framework describes problem solving in situations that involve physical or motor manipulations and trial and error.

Unique to humans, *higher mental functions* are cognitive processes acquired through learning and teaching. Higher mental functions are *deliberate, mediated, internalized* behaviors. When humans acquired higher mental functions, thinking became qualitatively different from that of the higher animals and evolved with the development of civilization. Higher mental functions include mediated perception, focused attention, deliberate memory, and logical thinking. When we distinguish between different colors, placing sky blue in a different category than turquoise blue, we are using mediated perception. Focused attention describes the ability to concentrate on *any* stimulus, whether or not it is exceptionally salient or striking. Deliberate memory refers to the use of memory strategies to remember something. Logical thinking involves the ability to solve problems mentally using logic and other strategies. All these higher mental functions are built upon lower mental functions in a culturally specific way. In current cognitive theories, many of the mental processes described by Vygotsky as higher mental functions are commonly referred to as *metacognitive*. Table 2.1 summarizes the difference between lower and higher mental functions.

Characteristics of Higher Mental Functions

Higher mental functions are deliberate in that they are controlled by the person and their use is based on thought and choice; they are used *on purpose*. The behaviors can be directed or focused on specific aspects of the environment, such as ideas, perceptions, and images, while ignoring other inputs. Young children lacking deliberateness react to the loudest noise or the most colorful picture. When children acquire higher mental functions, they direct their behavior to the aspects of the environment most pertinent to solving a problem. These aspects may not necessarily be the most perceptually obvious or noticeable (see Table 2.2).

Table 2.1.   Lower and higher mental functions

Lower Mental Functions	Higher Mental Functions
humans and higher animals	humans only
Sensation Reactive attention Spontaneous or associative memory Sensorimotor intelligence	Mediated perception Focused attention Deliberate memory Logical thinking

Table 2.2.   Examples of nondeliberate and deliberate mental behaviors

Nondeliberate Behavior	Deliberate Behavior
Cannot find a hidden figure in a picture because she searches in a unsystematic way or is distracted by other pictures	Searches for hidden figure in a systematic and deliberate way, ignoring other distracting figures
Cannot listen to the teacher when other children are talking	Listens to the teacher and blocks out distracting noises
Begins building with blocks that are nearest without regard to the structure being built	Begins building with blocks using a mental plan, so blocks that will be best for the future structure are chosen

Mediation is the use of certain signs or symbols in mental processing. It involves using something else to represent behavior or objects in the environment. The signs or symbols can be universal or specific to a small group, such as a family or classroom, or they can be specific to a particular person. For example, a stop sign or red light is a universal sign for stopping forward motion and is understood the world around. A teacher might use three fingers and a raised arm to stand for "Stop what you are doing" in his classroom. A child might use a personal mediator like "Daddy won't let me" to prevent or stop a certain action. Categories used in classifying objects also mediate our thinking, for example, classifying cats as a kind of animal (see Table 2.3).

Internalized behaviors exist in a person's mind and may not be observable. Internalization happens when external behaviors "grow into the mind," maintaining the same structure, focus, and function as their external manifestations (Vygotsky & Luria, 1930/1993). Adding a group of numbers using your fingers is an external behavior. Adding the numbers in your head is basically the same behavior, but it is internal.

In young children, most behaviors are external and visible. When young children are beginning the process of internalization, we can see the roots of higher mental functions in their overt actions, such as attempts to control memory by chanting or singing something repeatedly to themselves. Older children possessing deliberate memory may not show any overt strategies.

The Development of Higher Mental Functions

Vygotsky believed that higher mental functions develop in a specific way:

1. They are dependent on lower mental functions.
2. They are determined by the cultural context.
3. They develop from a shared to an individual function.
4. They involve internalization of a tool.

Table 2.3.   Examples of nonmediated and mediated behaviors

Nonmediated Behavior	Mediated Behavior
Trying to remember a complicated dance pattern you have just watched	Saying the names of the steps to yourself, such as "two right, three left, kick, kick"
Trying to visually estimate the number of items	Counting the items
Blurting out your comment after the teacher's question	Holding up your hand as a sign that you are ready to answer the question

Building on Lower Mental Functions

Higher mental functions are built upon lower mental functions that have developed to a specific level. Two-year-old Elena cannot remember all the words to "Itsy Bitsy Spider" because her spontaneous memory has not sufficiently developed. Presently, her ability to remember deliberately is primarily limited by the immaturity of the underlying lower mental functions, not by the absence of specific strategies.

When higher mental functions develop, a fundamental reorganization of lower mental functions occurs. From then on, children utilize higher mental functions more frequently, and while lower mental functions do not disappear completely, they are used less and less. For example, as children acquire language, they begin to remember in words rather than images or sensations. By the time we are adults, almost everything we remember is encoded in words.

The Influence of Cultural Context

Culture affects both the essence of the higher mental functions and the way mental functions are acquired. A classic example of this is found in Luria's studies of classification in the 1930s. Luria found that the classification system used by people who do not have formal schooling is quite different from those who do. People without formal schooling use an experience-based system of classification that depends on where they have encountered the objects. When asked which object does not belong—apples, watermelon, pears, or plate—they are likely to say all of the objects go together. Since people with formal schooling develop more abstract ways of categorizing, such as fruit and nonfruit, they are likely to exclude plates from the group. Luria's findings have been recently confirmed in several cross-cultural studies (Ceci, 1991).

The acquisition of higher mental functions also depends on the cultural context. Abstract thinking, such as using numbers, is learned in a different way depending on cultural background. In some African cultures children use their hands in a specific rhythm to help them add, in parts of Asia they use an abacus and in some North American classrooms, children count using Cuisinaire rods. The children in all three cultures learn the same mental skills but in different ways. Individuals may have the same higher mental functions, but the paths to their development may be different.

Moving from Shared to Individual Functions

Higher mental functions first exist in shared activity between two people. The child and her teacher share the mental process of planning a day's schedule of homework. The child uses the teacher's plan so that both are participating. As the child begins to appropriate a higher mental function, the child applies it independently. High school students usually do not need the teacher's help in planning homework priorities.

To acquire higher mental functions, the child must have already learned the basic mental tools of her culture. Mental tools are what children use to modify and restructure lower mental functions into higher mental functions. Mental tools, such as language, will reorganize the child's lower mental functions. We will discuss several tools and their relationship to higher mental functions in the chapters that follow.

Individual Differences in the Development of Mental Functions

Lower Mental Functions

Vygotsky believed that lower mental functions were culture-free, or independent of any cultural context. They seem to be part of our biological heritage. All people can solve sensorimotor problems regardless of whether they live in Papua, New Guinea or the United States. Lower mental functions depend primarily on maturation and growth and not on any particular type of instruction. However, all people do not develop the same level of lower mental functions. The problem may be organic. Children with certain learning disabilities lack some aspects of lower mental functions. Sensorimotor stimulation, the opportunity to manipulate objects and explore the environment, also affects lower mental functions. Extreme deprivation can lead to individual differences, especially in the first years of life, when lower mental functions are developing.

Higher Mental Functions

Individual differences in higher mental functions may be influenced by factors described above, but there are other contributing factors. One factor is the quality of language environment. Opportunities to hear and practice language will directly influence the future development of higher mental functions.

Another factor is social context. Some social contexts are more conducive to the development of higher mental functions. Vygotsky insisted that formal schooling was one of the most beneficial social contexts. Some aspects of higher mental functions can be learned only by going to school. The development of taxonomic categories (mammal, carnivore) is an example of "schooled" behavior. However, a child's informal experiences may be very different from those taught at school, especially when the child's culture is different from the mainstream culture. Most likely, white, middle-class children will have an informal context that is quite similar to that found in most schools in the United States. For them, the process of developing higher mental functions builds upon their previous accomplishments.

Children from other cultural backgrounds have varying degrees of similarity between school and their other social contexts. The degree of dissimilarity will influence how much mental restructuring must occur before the child can acquire the higher mental function presented in school. This is an important point for parents and educators to understand.

Vygotsky and Luria were very interested in the way that children with disabilities acquired higher mental functions. They believed that most children are capable of acquiring higher mental functions, but the path of development is different for children with disabilities. The external supports and the shared activities must be modified to stress the child's strengths. A discussion of Vygotsky's views on special education encompasses an entire set of writings and books and cannot be described in sufficient detail here. Both Vygotsky and Luria have contributed much to our understanding of learning in special education. For more information see the related references at the end of this chapter.

For Further Reading

Vygotsky, L. S., & Luria, A. R. (1993). *Studies in the history of behavior: Ape, primitive, and child.* Hillsdale, NJ: Lawrence Erlbaum. (Original work published in 1930).

Wertsch, J. V. (1985). *Vygotsky and the social formation of mind.* Cambridge: Harvard University Press.

Wertsch, J. V. (1991a). *Voices of the mind: A sociocultural approach to mediated action.* Cambridge: Harvard University Press.

Zukow-Goldring, P., & Ferko, K. R. (1994). An ecological approach to the emergence of lexicon: Socializing attention. In V. John-Steiner, C. P. Panofsky, & L. W. Smith, (Eds.), *Sociocultural approaches to language and literacy: An interactionist perspective.* Cambridge: Cambridge University Press.

Special Education References

Berk, L. E., & Winsler, A. (1995). Scaffolding children's learning: Vygotsky and early childhood education. *NAEYC Research and Practice Series, 7.* Washington, DC: National Association for the Education of Young Children.

Cole, M. (Ed.). (1978). *The selected writings of A. R. Luria.* White Plains, NY: M. E. Sharpe.

Evans, P. (1993). Some implications of Vygotsky's work for special education. In H. Daniels (Ed.), *Charting the agenda: Education activity after Vygotsky.* London: Routledge.

Gindis, B. (1995). The social/cultural implication of disability: Vygotsky's paradigm for special education. *Educational Psychologist,* 30(2), 77-81.

Vocate, D. R. (1987). *The theory of A. R. Luria: Functions of spoken language in the development of higher mental processes.* Hillsdale, NJ: Lawrence Erlbaum.

Vygotsky, L. S. (1993). *The collected works of L. S. Vygotsky: Fundamentals of Defectology (Abnormal Psychology and Learning Disabilities)* (Vol. II). New York: Plenum Press (Original works published 1920–1930).

CHAPTER 3

The Vygotskian Framework and Other Theories of Child Development

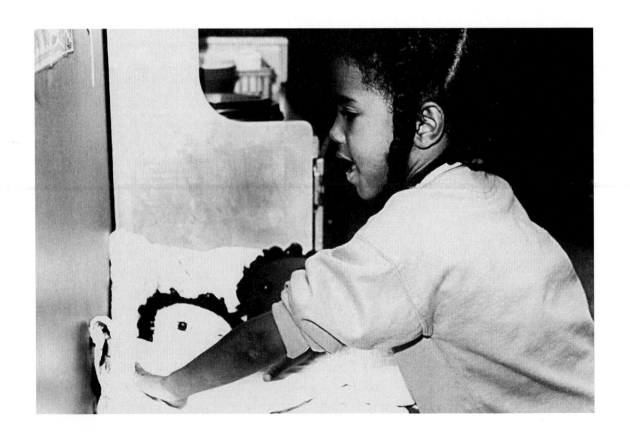

In this chapter, we will first compare Vygotsky's theory with other theories of child development and then give a general critique of the Vygotskian approach. These comparisons focus on the major principles of his Cultural-Historical Theory described in Chapter 1. More detailed comparisons between specific concepts appear in later chapters as each Vygotskian concept is introduced.

Vygotsky studied and commented on the work of constructivists (Piaget), behaviorists (Watson), Gestalt psychologists (Koffka), and psychoanalysts (Freud), as well as the work of educators (Montessori). Vygotskian theory also complements many of the ideas in information processing theory which was developed after his death.

Piaget's Constructivist Approach

Vygotsky was familiar with the early works of Jean Piaget such as *The Language and Thought of the Child* (1923/1926). In his book, *Thought and Language* (1934/1962), Vygotsky criticized the Piagetian perspective on the relationship between thought and language and proposed his own approach. Piaget accepted some of Vygotsky's criticisms and modified some of his later ideas, but this did not happen during Vygotsky's lifetime. The works of some of Vygotsky's students (e.g., Leont'ev) have more in common with Piaget than the works of Vygotsky himself. These similarities have caused many psychologists to erroneously consider the Vygotskian framework as part of Piaget's constructivist tradition.

Similarities

Both Piaget's and Vygotsky's theories are best known for their insights into the development of thought processes. Piaget placed thinking at the center of child development (Beilin, 1994). Although the bulk of Vygotsky's work was concerned with the development of thinking, Vygotsky had planned to study other areas of development that he considered equally important (such as emotions), but his early death did not allow him to complete this work.

Piaget and Vygotsky agree that a child's development is a series of qualitative changes that cannot be viewed as merely an expanding repertoire of skills and ideas. For Piaget, these changes occur in distinct stages (Ginsberg & Opper, 1988). Vygotsky, however, proposed a set of less well defined periods. He wrote primarily about the restructuring of the child's mind that takes place in the periods of transition from one stage to another and placed less emphasis on each stage's characteristics.

Both Piaget and Vygotsky believed that children are active in their acquisition of knowledge. This belief differentiates them from the proponents of behaviorism, who view learning as determined primarily by external (environmental) variables. Instead of seeing the child as a passive participant, a vessel waiting to be filled with knowledge, both Vygotsky and Piaget stress the active intellectual efforts that children make in order to learn.

Both theories describe the construction of knowledge in the mind. Piaget believed that young children's thinking is different from adults' and that the knowledge that children possess is not *just* an incomplete copy of what adults have. Vygotsky and Piaget agree that children construct their own understandings and that with age and experience these understandings are restructured.

In his later writings, Piaget acknowledges the role of social transmission in development (Beilin, 1994), social transmission being the passing of the accumulated wisdom of the culture from one generation to the next. Vygotsky also believed in the importance of culture in transmitting knowledge. Piaget, however, believed that social transmission influences primarily the content of knowledge, whereas for Vygotsky social transmission plays a much greater role; it influences not only content but the very nature and essence of the thinking process.

Finally, for both theorists the elements of mature thought are quite similar. Piaget describes formal operational thinking as abstract, logical, reflective, and hypothetical-deductive. Vygotsky's higher mental functions involve logic, abstract thinking, and self-reflection.

The emphasis on abstract, logical thinking has led some psychologists to criticize Piaget and Vygotsky for being Eurocentric because they place a higher value on those mental processes that are more prevalent in Western, technologically advanced societies (Berk, 1994; Ginsberg & Opper, 1988; Wertsch & Tulviste, 1994). While Vygotsky did place more emphasis on logical thought, he believed that all humans are capable of developing it, given exposure, and that the lack of development of logic in a particular culture was due to the fact that it was not "useful" in that culture.

Differences

For Piaget, intellectual development has a universal nature independent of the child's cultural context. Thus, all children reach the stage of formal operations at around the age of 14. For Vygotsky, the cultural context determines the very type of cognitive processes that emerge. Cultures that do not extensively employ formal reasoning would not foster the development of formal operations in their young. Vygotsky's ideas have been supported by the data obtained in cross-cultural studies of societies where children do not develop formal operations (Jahoda,1980; Laboratory of Comparative Human Cognition, 1983; Scribner, 1977). Much of the research of some of Piaget's students (Perret-Clermont, Perret, & Bell, 1991) also stresses the contribution of cultural context.

While Piaget emphasizes the role of the child's interactions with physical objects in developing mature forms of thinking (Beilin, 1994), Vygotsky focuses on the child's interactions with people. For Piaget, people are of secondary importance, while the objects and the child's actions on objects are of primary importance. Peers may create cognitive dissonance, but they are not an integral part of the learning process. For Vygotsky, a child's actions on objects are beneficial for development only as long as they are included in a social context and mediated by communication with others.

For Piaget, language is more a by-product of intellectual development than one of its roots (Beilin, 1994). Language can increase the "power of thought in range and rapidity" by representing actions, liberating thought from space and time, or organizing actions (Piaget & Inhelder, 1969, p. 86). However, the way a child talks merely reflects the present stage of the child's cognition; it has no impact on the progression from one stage to another. For Vygotsky, language plays a major role in cognitive development and forms the very core of the child's mental functions.

Piaget views the child as an "independent discoverer" who learns about the world on his own. Vygotsky argues that there is no such thing as completely independent discovery for children who grow up in human society. Instead, a child's learning takes place in a cultural context, and both things to be discovered and the means of discovery are products of human history and culture.

Piaget believed that only the discoveries children make independently reflect their current intellectual status. Knowledge of how children acquire or apply knowledge that is transmitted by adults is not relevant in determining a child's developmental level. Vygotsky, in contrast, believed that appropriation of cultural knowledge plays the key role in a child's cognitive development. Therefore, a child's shared performance is as valuable for determining her intellectual status as independent performance.

The effect of learning on development is viewed differently by Piaget and Vygotsky. For Piaget, a child's current developmental status determines his ability to learn and cannot be changed by the learning itself. Accordingly, all teaching should be adjusted to the existing cognitive abilities of a child. For Vygotsky, the relationship between learning and development is more complex. For certain knowledge or content and for certain ages, one step in learning may mean two steps in development. In other cases, learning and development proceed at a more even pace. However, teaching should be always aimed at the child's emerging skills, not at the existing ones.

Behaviorist Theories

In Russia of the twenties and thirties, when Vygotsky did most of his writing, behaviorism in its various forms was one of the most influential psychological theories. Vygotsky lived in the epoch of early behaviorism represented by John B. Watson (1924/1970) and was not familiar with later developments within this framework. Although Vygotsky disagreed strongly with behaviorists, the influence of this theory is evident in his language.

Similarities

Like the behaviorists, Vygotsky favored the use of objective methods in psychology. His approach was not purely speculative but was based on observations, measurements, and experiments. Vygotsky criticized the use of introspection as an experimental method, as did the behaviorists.

Although Vygotsky stressed unique features of the human mind, he also recognized that humans and animals have certain common behaviors. Like the behaviorists, Vygotsky believed that animals and humans are part of the same evolutionary continuum, not completely different forms.

Another similarity of the behaviorists and Vygotsky is their mutual interest in learning. Behaviorism and the Vygotskian framework both focus on the learning process, although they approach it from different directions.

Differences

Unlike early behaviorists, Vygotsky was not satisfied with measuring only overt behaviors. Vygotsky did not believe that thinking could be understood by considering only those behaviors that can be measured and observed by another person. He always tried to explain overt behaviors using inferences based on broader theoretical categories. Later theories of behaviorism also use concepts that are inferred from overt behaviors but cannot be directly observed (Horowitz, 1994).

The major disagreement Vygotsky had with the behaviorists was on the nature of the "stimuli" that trigger certain behaviors in animals and humans. Behaviorists assert that the relationship between stimuli and behavior is the same for all organisms. For Vygotsky, the fundamental difference between humans and animals lies in the fact that humans are able to respond to stimuli that they generate for themselves. By responding to these specifically created stimuli, or "tools," humans actually gain control over their own behavior (see Figure 3.1).

In addition, Vygotsky opposed Watson's view of speech as no different from other overt behaviors. Watson believed that thinking was just "silent speech." For Vygotsky, speech plays a unique role in the process of mental development, and thinking is substantially different from speech in its form and function (see Chapter 8).

The views of Vygotsky and the behaviorists on the relationship between learning and development also differ. Behaviorists do not distinguish between these two processes and do not address development as a separate concept. From this fact Vygotsky concluded that behaviorists believe that learning *is* development. Behaviorists, indeed,

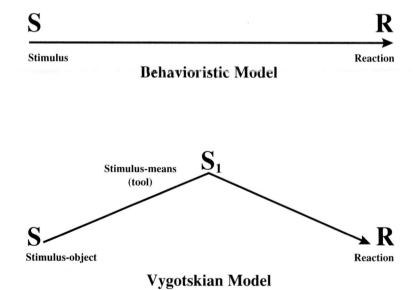

Figure 3.1.   Comparison of behaviorist and Vygotskian views of behavior

maintain that a developing child is always the same child but becomes more knowledgeable and skillful as a result of learning. For behaviorists, there are no qualitative changes in mental structures; learning is simply cumulative. Vygotsky argues that there are qualitative changes not explained by growth in the number of things a child knows. He states that certain learnings can reorganize and qualitatively change the structure of thought. For example, when children acquire language, they begin to think in words, thereby changing both their sensorimotor thinking and problem-solving abilities.

Finally, Vygotsky and the behaviorists differ on the idea of construction of knowledge. Behaviorists see the child as relatively passive, with knowledge being a product of associations strengthened through reinforcement. Vygotsky claims that children construct knowledge and are active in acquiring knowledge. Children act based on these mental structures and understandings. For behaviorists, the environment (including physical objects and other people) is in control of the child's thoughts and actions, selecting the appropriate ones and increasing them through reinforcement. In contrast, Vygotsky argues that the acquisition of knowledge and tools give the child a means to control her own thoughts and actions.

Information Processing Theory

Information processing theory (e.g., Atkinson & Shiffrin, 1968) was developed long after Vygotsky's death. Even so, many of the concepts that Vygotsky developed predicted and are consistent with the research findings of information processing theory.

Similarities

Both the Vygotskian framework and information processing theory stress the importance of metacognition in mature thinking and problem solving. In both theories metacognition includes the concepts of self-regulation, self-reflection, evaluation, and monitoring.

In addition, information processing theorists and Vygotsky agree that the child must make a mental effort to learn. There is nothing passive about this process. Furthermore, new learning is not merely added to existing structures but modifies present knowledge. Vygotsky speaks of comprehension as a dialogue in which the child communicates with the teacher or the author of a text to build new meanings rather than simply copying existing ones.

Finally, information processing theorists and Vygotsky stress cognitive processes and semantics, or the meaning of words. Both theories place attention, memory, and metacognition at the center of the learning process.

Differences

Information processing theory is not really a developmental theory. It describes processing at different ages but does not explain why children are better at it as they grow older. On the other hand, Vygotsky is primarily concerned with how these processes develop and how they are taught to children.

Since information processing theory uses the computer as the primary analogue for the human mind, the social context and the way it forms thinking processes are not considered. Culture influences input—knowledge and facts—but not the method of processing information. For Vygotsky, culture influences both the content of thinking and the way humans process information; it affects the nature of attention, memory, and metacognition. For example, Vygotskian researchers found that primacy and recency effects, which are described by information processing theorists as universal phenomena in memory, are influenced by the type of schooling children have. Whether children remember only the last thing they heard (recency effect) or the first and the last things they heard (primacy and recency effects) depends on the culture they belong to (Valsiner, 1988).

Finally, emotional and motivational aspects of learning are ignored by information processing theorists. Vygotskians believe that emotions and motivation are important in the learning process. Children learn best when they feel emotionally engaged in learning activities. Leont'ev (1977/1978) did extensive research to identify what makes an activity motivating and beneficial to young children (his research is summarized in Chapter 5).

Critique of the Vygotskian Approach

Because Vygotsky died before many of the ideas he proposed were researched and many of the questions he posed were answered, his writings do not form a coherent, well-organized theory. Consequently, his ideas about some areas of development, such as the relationship between emotions and learning, are not fully explained, elaborated, or demonstrated empirically.

One common criticism is that Vygotsky placed too much emphasis on the role of speech in cognitive development and did not adequately explore how other types of symbolic representations contribute to higher mental functions. Later research completed by Zaporozhets and Venger showed how nonverbal cultural tools promote the development of perception and thinking in young children (Zaporozhets, 1959/1977; Venger, 1969/1977).

A second criticism is that Vygotsky placed too much emphasis on the role that others play in shared activity and not enough on what the child must do to be an active participant. It was in part in response to this criticism that his colleague Leont'ev (1977/1978) developed his "activity theory" which stresses the child's active participation in shared activity.

As we shall see in the following chapters, the Vygotskian framework provides a view of the developing child that is distinct from the ideas in Western psychology. The framework has the potential to help us understand the learning and teaching process in a more precise way.

For Further Reading

Parke, R. D.; Ornstein; P. A.; Rieser, J. J.; & Zahn-Waxler, C. (Eds.). (1994). *A century of developmental psychology*. Washington, DC: American Psychological Association.

Strategies for Development and Learning

In this section we describe general strategies for promoting development and learning. The concepts presented in the first section of the book are discussed as they apply to the learning/teaching process. There are three chapters in this section:

Chapter 4 The Zone of Proximal Development

Chapter 5 Developmental Accomplishments and Leading Activity: Infants and Toddlers

Chapter 6 Developmental Accomplishments and Leading Activity: Preschool, Kindergarten, and Primary Grades

The Zone of Proximal Development

Both the acquisition of a specific cultural tool and further mental development depend on whether or not that tool lies within the child's zone of proximal development. Vygotsky considered the ZPD a strategy for development and learning.

Defining the Zone of Proximal Development

The *zone of proximal development,* or *ZPD,* one of the most well known of all of Vygotsky's concepts, is a way of conceptualizing the relationship between learning and development. Vygotsky chose the word *zone* because he conceived development not as a point on a scale, but as a continuum of behaviors or degrees of maturation. By describing the zone as proximal (next to, close to), he meant that the zone is limited by those behaviors that will develop in the *near* future. *Proximal* refers not to all possible behaviors that will eventually emerge, but to those closest to emergence at any given time.

Independent Performance and Assisted Performance

For Vygotsky, development of a behavior occurs on two levels which form the boundaries of the ZPD. The lower level is the child's *independent performance,* what the child knows and can do alone. The higher level is the maximum the child can reach with help and is called *assisted performance.* Between maximally assisted performance and independent performance lie varying degrees of partially assisted performances (see Figure 4.1).

The skills and behaviors represented in the ZPD are dynamic and constantly changing. What a child does with some assistance today is what the child will do independently tomorrow. What requires maximum support and assistance today will be something the child can do with minimal help tomorrow. Thus, the assisted performance level will change as the child develops.

In education and psychology, we have traditionally focused on what is developed or achieved by independent performance only. For example, we say that if 5-year-old Susan correctly adds $2 + 2$ by herself, then she can add. Frank has learned to make the letter *n* only when he can draw it on his own. If there is a prompt by an adult, for instance, if the teacher reminds Frank that "an *n* has one hump," then we say that the child has not developed or doesn't know the information yet. Vygotsky maintains that the level of independent performance is an important index of development, but he argues that it is not sufficient to completely describe development.

The level of assisted performance includes behaviors performed with the help of or in interaction with another person, either an adult or peer. This interaction may involve giving hints and clues, rephrasing questions, asking the child to restate what has been said, asking the child what he understands, demonstrating the task or a portion of it, and so on. The interaction can also take the form of indirect help, such as setting up the environment to facilitate practicing a specific set of skills. For example, a teacher might provide labeled sorting trays to encourage classification. Assisted performance also includes interaction and talking to others who are present or imaginary, such as

Figure. 4.1.   The zone of proximal development

explaining something to a peer. Thus, a child's level of assisted performance includes any situation in which there are improvements in the child's mental activities as a result of social interaction. The specific kinds of social interactions that result in advances in mental development are described in Chapters 5 and 6.

Dynamics of the ZPD

The ZPD is not static but shifts as the child attains a higher level of thinking and knowledge (see Figure 4.2). Thus, development involves a sequence of constantly changing

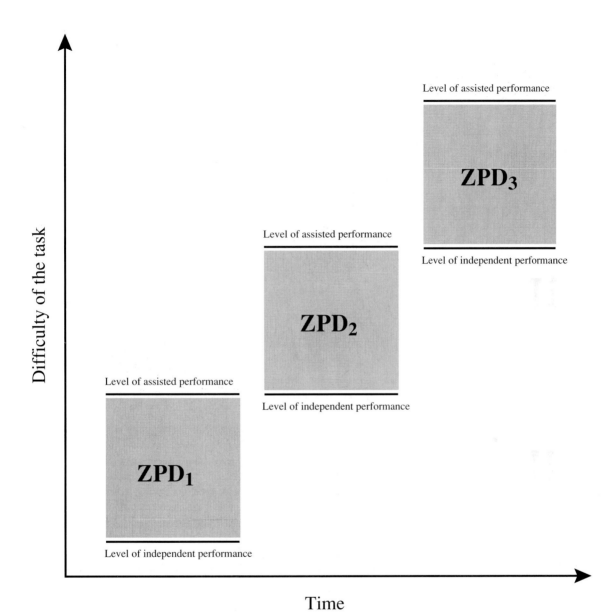

Figure. 4.2.   The dynamic nature of the ZPD

zones. With each shift, the child becomes capable of learning more and more complex concepts and skills. What the child did only with assistance yesterday becomes the
level of independent performance today. Then, as the child tackles more difficult
tasks, a new level of assisted performance emerges. This cycle is repeated over and over

again, as the child climbs his way to complete acquisition of a body of knowledge, skill, strategy, discipline, or behavior.

The zone of proximal development is different for different children. Some children require all possible assistance to make even small gains in the learning. Other children make huge leaps with much less assistance.

At the same time, the size of the zone of proximal development for one child may vary from one area to another or at different times in the learning process. A highly verbal child may not have trouble acquiring concepts in reading comprehension, for example, but have great difficulty with long division. Vygotskians would say that the child needs more assistance in one area than another. In addition, at various times in the process of learning, children respond to different types of assistance. If Mary has been counting only a few weeks, she may need more assistance closer to her level of independent performance than she does 3 months later, after she has been counting for several months. At that time the ZPD will be larger and the amount that she can do with assistance will be greater.

Using the ZPD to Study Development

Vygotsky's approach focuses on the child "to be" or "the future child" rather than on the "present child," what she is like at this moment. As Leont'ev stated after Vygotsky's death, "American researchers are constantly seeking to discover how the child came to be what he is; we in the USSR are striving to discover not how the child came to be what he is, but how he can become what he not yet is" (Bronfenbrenner, 1977, p. 528). Because of this focus, the emphasis in the Vygotskian paradigm is on the higher level of the ZPD or what the child will be in time.

But how can we study something that doesn't yet exist? If we wait until a certain concept or skill emerges, we will be studying today's child, not tomorrow's! What we need is a way to study the process that occurs between the current state and tomorrow's state.

One of the innovations of the Vygotskian approach is the research method of *double stimulation,* or the *microgenetic method,* as it is better known in American psychology (Valsiner, 1989). In this method the researcher studies the child as new concepts or skills emerge. The researcher designs the hints, cues, and other assistance to reveal not just what the child learns but *how* the child learns. A child is given a novel learning task, and the researcher monitors which elements of the context (hints, prompts, materials, cues, and interactions) are used by the child. Thus, the researcher provides assistance at the higher level of the ZPD and monitors the child's progress within the ZPD (Gal'perin, 1969).

Vygotsky insisted that the entire ZPD be used to determine the child's developmental level because it reveals (a) skills on the edge of emergence, and (b) the limits of the child's development at this specific time.

The child's behavior in assisted performance reveals the behaviors that are on the verge of emerging. However, if we use only independent performance to find out where a child is, what she knows and can do, then those skills that are on the edge of emergence will not be apparent. Two children whose independent performance is on the same level may have very different developmental characteristics because their zones of proximal development differ. For example, neither Teresa nor Linda can walk across a balance beam. Both of them stand on the end and stare down the beam. The teacher holds out his hand to assist each girl's performance. Although each is given the same teacher support, Teresa can only stand on the balance beam holding the teacher's hand tightly while Linda walks across the beam easily. Independent performance alone is misleading in this example. When we see how the two girls respond to assistance, we can tell that they are at very different levels.

The ZPD is not limitless; a child cannot be taught anything at any given time. Assisted performance is the *maximum* level at which a child can perform today. Children cannot be taught skills or behaviors that exceed their ZPD. In the above example, Teresa and Linda, no matter what support the teacher gave that day, could not be taught to do a handstand on the beam.

When a skill is outside of the ZPD, children generally ignore, fail to use, or incorrectly use that skill. By observing children's reactions teachers will know if the assistance provided falls within the ZPD. Teachers must carefully note which prompts, clues, hints, books, activities, or peer cooperative activities have a desired effect on the child's learning. Teachers should not be afraid to try a higher level, but teachers need to listen to the child by paying attention to the child's reaction to attempts at the higher level of the ZPD.

Implications for Learning/Teaching

The term *learning/teaching* is currently used as a translation of the Russian word *obuchenyie*. *Obuchenyie* describes both a child's learning and the teacher's teaching of knowledge and skills. It includes the contribution of both the learner and the teacher and implies that both are active in this process. In contrast, in Western conceptions of education, learning tends to describe only what the pupil does, while words like *teaching, training,* and *educating* describe primarily the teacher's role. Thus the term learning/teaching more accurately represents Vygotsky's meaning than either the words learning or teaching alone.

The zone of proximal development has three important implications for learning/teaching:

1. How to assist a child in performing a task
2. How to assess children
3. How to determine what is developmentally appropriate

Assisting Performance

It is common to think of the assisted performance level of the zone of proximal development in terms of expert-novice interactions, in which one person has more knowledge than the other. In this type of interaction, most commonly occurring in direct teaching, it is the expert's responsibility to provide support and direct the interaction so that the novice can acquire the necessary behavior. These expert-novice interactions can be informal, as when children and parents or siblings interact (Rogoff, 1990).

Vygotsky's conception of ZPD, however, is much broader than the expert-novice interaction, extending to all socially shared activities. Also, not all of the assistance used by the child is assistance intentionally provided by an adult. Vygotsky believed that the child can start performing on a higher level of a ZPD through any type of social interaction: interaction with peers as equals, with imaginary partners, or with children at other developmental levels (Newman & Holzman, 1993). For example, 3-year-old Benny cannot sit still during a story. The teacher tries to provide different types of assistance to help him focus. She calls out his name, places her hand on his shoulder, and signals to him nonverbally. In spite of these efforts, Benny continues to wiggle and look around the room. Later that day, Benny is playing school with a group of friends. Tony sits in a chair and "reads" the book just like the teacher, while Benny and several other children "pretend" to be students and listen. Benny sits and listens focusing his attention for 4 to 5 minutes. Benny is practicing the same behavior that the teacher desired, focused attention. The ability to concentrate for a short time is within his ZPD, but we can see that he requires a particular type of assistance, that of play and peers. With the assistance of his peers, he is able to perform at the higher levels of his ZPD, but with the teacher he is not able to do so. We will discuss in Chapter 10 why play is so useful in helping children to move through a ZPD.

Assessing Children's Abilities

The idea of ZPD has direct implications for assessing what children know and can do. Instead of limiting assessment only to what children can do independently, we should include what they can do with different levels of assistance. Teachers should note how children use their help as well as what hints are the most useful. This technique, often called "dynamic assessment," has great potential for improving and expanding authentic classroom assessment (Cronbach, 1990; McAfee & Leong, 1994; Spector, 1992).

By using the ZPD in assessment, not only do we have a more accurate estimate of the child's abilities, but we have a more flexible way of assessing children. Teachers can rephrase a question, pose it differently, or encourage the child to show what she knows. Using the ZPD, we get at the child's best understanding.

Defining Developmentally Appropriate Practice

The idea of the zone of proximal development broadens the scope of "developmentally appropriate" practice. What is developmentally appropriate is currently defined by the child's independent achievements, by the processes and skills that have fully developed (Bredecamp, 1992). It does not include the level of assisted performance and emerging processes and skills. Thus, teachers are likely to wait until desired behavior emerges spontaneously before providing activities that encourage it. As a result, children only have learning opportunities at what Vygotsky considers the lower level of their ZPD.

The concept of ZPD expands the idea of what is developmentally appropriate to include things the child can learn with assistance. Vygotsky argues that the most effective teaching is aimed at the higher level of a child's ZPD. Teachers should provide activities just beyond what the child can do on his own but within what the child can do with assistance. Thus, the learning/teaching dialogue proceeds slightly ahead of the child's status at any given time. For example, if adults only provided language stimulation geared to the child's actual speech and not at a level slightly higher, then they would only use baby talk with toddlers and never speak in full sentences. In actual practice, of course, both parents and teachers intuitively add more information and use more complex grammar than the toddler is currently capable of producing. As a result, the child learns more complex grammar and expands her vocabulary.

Another example of how we intuitively use the level of assisted performance is when dealing with the conflicts that naturally arise between young children. When 2 ½ year olds are fighting, the teacher points out each child's feelings even though the children may not yet be able to take another person's perspective. Few teachers would want to wait until perspective-taking skills emerge naturally when children are 4 and 5 years of age before asking students to use them.

Vygotsky emphasizes that the child should practice what he can do independently and, at the same time, be exposed to things at the higher levels of the ZPD. Both levels are developmentally appropriate. Teachers must be sensitive to the child's reaction to the support and assistance provided in the ZPD. If the child accepts the teacher's support, then the teacher has hit within the ZPD. If a child ignores help, and still cannot perform at the higher level of the ZPD as expected, then the teacher needs to rethink the support. Perhaps the skill is outside this child's zone or the type of assistance provided is not useful and should be modified. The ZPD helps teachers look at what support to provide and how the child reacts in a more sensitive way.

Using the ZPD to Teach

Several researchers have taken the idea of the ZPD and tried to delineate more specifically what goes on within it. Vygotsky was rather vague about exactly how the child reaches the upper limit of the zone. From among the many psychologists who have discussed the ZPD, we have chosen a few who present more detail and whose works help teachers in the practical job of teaching children. Zaporozhets (1986); Wood, Bruner, & Ross (1976); Newman, Griffin, & Cole (1989); Newman & Holzman (1993); Tharp & Gallimore (1988); Cazden (1981); and Rogoff (1986) have all described what goes on within the ZPD in slightly different ways. Each conception adds to our understanding of the ZPD and how it works, giving guidance to teachers who want to use the ZPD to improve their teaching.

Amplification

Zaporozhets (1986) has coined the term *amplification* to describe how to use the child's entire current ZPD to the fullest. The idea of amplification is the opposite of acceleration or speeding up the children's development. Acceleration, Zaporozhets maintains, does not lead to optimum development because it teaches skills that the child is not prepared to learn, because they lie far outside her ZPD. You can teach children some things outside of their ZPD, but this skill or content knowledge will exist as an isolated bit of information that will not be integrated into the children's world view. Consequently, acceleration does not have a positive impact on developmental accomplishments of the next period. For example, after much training, children as young as 3 years old can be taught to locate the letters on the typewriter. This learning, however, does not lead to the development of written speech because it is outside the child's ZPD. Another example can be seen when children memorize the multiplication table before they understand addition. They can be taught to do this, but they will not be able to use it meaningfully to solve problems.

Amplification, on the other hand, builds upon strengths and increases development but does not reach outside the ZPD. Amplification assists behaviors on the edge of emergence, using the tools and assisted performance within the child's ZPD. For example, preschool children learn many things by manipulating objects. Manipulatives can be used to teach concepts such as number or classification, which form a part of theoretical reasoning at the next stage. Children can use manipulatives to understand physical relationships such as that between distance and speed. Children can use this knowledge later when they begin to reason about distance and speed in a more abstract way, when they are 9 or 10. Thus, teaching preschoolers the abstract formula for the relationship between speed and distance would not be appropriate.

Scaffolding

Wood, Bruner, & Ross (1976) propose that the expert provide *scaffolding* within the ZPD to enable the novice to perform at a higher level. With scaffolding the task itself is not changed, but what the learner initially does is made easier with assistance. Gradually, the level of assistance decreases as the learner takes more responsibility for performance of the task. For example, if a child is to count 10 objects, the initial task asked of the child is to count 10 objects (not 3 or 5 or 7). At the level of maximum scaffolding, the teacher counts out loud with the child, holding the child's finger as she points to each object. At this point, the teacher has most of the responsibility for counting, while the child follows his action. The teacher then gradually begins to withdraw support, just as the scaffolding of a building is taken away as the walls are capable of standing alone. The next time the child counts, the teacher does not say the numbers but still helps her point. Then the teacher may stop pointing at the objects, allowing the child to both point and count on her own.

Wood, Bruner, & Ross (1976) suggest that what the expert does when providing scaffolding may vary. Sometimes the adult might direct attention to an aspect that was forgotten; at other times the adult may actually model the correct manner of doing something. For scaffolding to be effective, however, the expert must enlist the child's interest:

> Reduce or simplify the number of steps required to solve the problem so the child can manage them, maintain the child's interest in pursuing the goal, point out the critical

features that show the difference between the child's performance and the ideal performance, control frustration, and demonstrate the idealized version of what the child is doing. (Wood, Bruner, & Ross, 1976, p. 60)

Bruner studied scaffolding primarily in the area of language acquisition. He points out that when young children are learning language, parents present the child with mature speech. Not all sentences are reduced to baby talk. However, parents vary the amount of contextual support they give. They restate, repeat the important words that have meaning, use gestures, and respond to the child's utterances by focusing on the meaning of the child's utterances and not the grammatical form. Adults maintain a dialogue with the child as if the child is another adult who understands everything. Parents act as if the child can understand, thus responding to the ZPD and not to the child's actual level of speech production. This is what Garvey called talking with "the future child" (Garvey, 1986, p. 331). Say that a child points to a tiger at the zoo and says, "Rrrrr," and the parent responds by saying, "Yes, that's a tiger. See her babies? She has three babies." The parent responds as if the child has produced the sentence "Look at the tiger." After repeated exposures to more mature language forms within the ZPD, children begin to acquire grammar. Bruner gave this support a specific name, the *Language Acquisition Support System,* or *LASS.*

At the beginning of the learning process, the adult provides more active interventions and greater amounts of scaffolding, directing more of the child's behavior than later in the process. As the child or novice learns, there is a shift in responsibility for the performance as the learner takes a greater role in producing the behavior. The task of the adult or teacher then becomes one of timing the removal of the scaffolding to enhance the child's successful independent performance of the final behavior. This shift in responsibility is what Bruner has called the "hand over principle" by which the child who was at first the spectator becomes a participant (Bruner, 1983, p. 60). The adult or expert hands over the task to the child. In summary, the idea of scaffolding clarifies that the following occurs within the ZPD:

1. The task is not made easier, but the amount of assistance is varied.
2. Responsibility for performances is transferred, or handed over, to the child as the child learns.

The ZPD as Construction Zone

Michael Cole and his colleagues (Newman, Griffin, & Cole, 1989), who worked with children in elementary school classrooms in California, describe the ZPD as a "construction zone." The teacher knows the goal of the task and has an idea of what the child's final performance will look like. The child does not have a full understanding of the goal or what the final performance will look like. The child constructs an image of what he thinks the teacher wants him to do. The teacher constructs an image of what the child understands, comparing this to the final performance. For example, 4-year-old Matthew is sorting a tray of seashells into big and small ones. Ms. Bien, his teacher, says, "How did you sort these? What kinds of groups did you make?" Matthew says, "Shells." Ms. Bien says, "Right, they are all shells, but this group is . . . " Matthew says, "White?" Ms. Bien says, "Well, some of them are white, but what about this pile?" She puts a sorting ring around the pile so it is more distinct. "What did you put over here?" She offers him a big shell and a small one and says, pointing to the big pile, "Which one goes in this pile?" "Oh," says Matthew, "those are big." Then he places the big shell in the correct pile. As you can see from this dialogue, Matthew is struggling to figure out what the teacher is asking him. The teacher keeps trying to redefine the question so she can find out whether or not Matthew was sorting by size or just made two piles arbitrarily.

Newman, Griffin, & Cole (1989) emphasize the importance of the dialogue between the child and teacher. Internalization is not a mirror of external events, nor is it a result of the child acting in isolation. There must be action by the teacher and by the child. In using the ZPD the teacher must encourage the child to act. The teacher must ask questions, probe, and discover what and how the child understands. The teacher thereby reveals, for his own understanding, what the child's mental processes are. By assessing these as he teaches, the ZPD is measured.

In summary, Cole and his colleagues have added the following ideas to our understanding of the ZPD:

1. Both the child and the teacher struggle to understand each other within the zone. The child struggles to try to understand the task and the teacher. The teacher struggles to understand the child's thinking.
2. Knowledge is co-constructed by the child and the adult within the zone.
3. No matter how many times we describe the goal of instruction, the child will probably not fully understand it until he has learned the particular concept, skill, or strategy.

Performance and Competence

Another way of looking at the learning that occurs within the ZPD is the idea that children at the upper level can perform the task, but not be competent at it. This is what Cazden (1981) terms "performance comes before competence." Children do not need full knowledge or full understanding of the task before we teach it to them. Competence and understanding are acquired after the task has been performed a number of times. Linda is learning how to add numbers using the Cuisenaire rods. She can correctly line up the correct number of 1's and 5's to make 10, but she can't explain the process. Even when she repeats the teacher's explanation, you get the feeling that she is just repeating the words with little understanding. After a few more practices, the teacher's explanation dawns on her, and she says, "I get it!"

As long as the behavior is within the child's ZPD, the lack of complete understanding is not a problem. That understanding will come with continued dialogue and interaction with others.

Structuring Situations

Rogoff (1986, 1990) studied assisted performance in informal settings, including mother-toddler interactions and interactions between weaving teachers and apprentices in Mexico. Rogoff argues that the adult or expert grades or structures tasks into different levels or subgoals. These subgoals are then broken down further or are changed as the zone of proximal development is explored in the interaction between the participants. By choosing toys, equipment, materials, or tools, the expert limits and structures the task even before the learner appears. Later, as the ZPD is explored, the expert adjusts the task, breaking it into smaller, more manageable tasks that the learner can do. In addition the expert may build redundancy into the interaction, repeating directions or modeling actions several times. In teaching counting, the teacher may limit the number of objects to count or choose objects of only one type to help structure the task. If the child cannot count 10 objects, the teacher may drop back to counting only 5 objects. Structuring aids the learner in performing at the highest level of the ZPD. Rogoff emphasizes the importance of the changes the expert must make to assist performance.

Rogoff (1986, 1990) also notes that the changes in adult structuring and support follow the learner's lead and are not arbitrarily imposed based on the content of the material or an abstract idea of how the information should be taught. Teaching begins with the child's independent level of performance, and it is only by knowing where each child is that we can begin.

In summary, Rogoff's contribution to our understanding of the ZPD relates to the expert's role:

1. The expert breaks goals into subgoals and manages the interactions accordingly.

2. The expert responds to the learner's initial level of performance.

Four Stages of the ZPD

Tharp and Gallimore (1988) directed the Kamehameha Elementary Education Program (KEEP) in Hawaii and worked with elementary aged children. They have proposed a four-stage description of the ZPD that goes beyond the definition commonly used by most researchers in the Vygotskian framework. The most distinctive aspect of their approach is the concept of performance in the ZPD as a circular, recursive process, rather than a linear one, with the following stages:

Stage 1. Performance is assisted by more capable others.
Stage 2. Performance is assisted by self.
Stage 3. Performance is developed, automatized, and "fossilized."
Stage 4. De-automatization of performance leads to recursion back through the ZPD. (Tharp & Gallimore, 1988, p. 35)

Like Cole and his colleagues, Tharp and Gallimore state that initially children have a very limited understanding of what they are learning. Therefore, at stage 1 the child's response is "acquiescent or imitative" (p. 33). The child is able to perform the task but does not fully understand how she got the answer. At this stage the most helpful types of interactions are modeling, contingent management (setting a pattern of rewards), feeding back (letting children know how close their behavior is to the target), instructing (giving direct instructions about strategies), questioning (asking leading questions), and cognitive structuring (providing explanatory and belief structures that organize and give meaning). During this stage, the teacher guides performance, tailoring assistance and providing new opportunities for transfer. Stage 1 has been accomplished when the learner takes responsibility for the structuring of the task.

In stage 2, performance is assisted by the learner herself. This is a transition stage because performance is not fully internalized, developed, or automatized. The child issues self-instructions, controlling behavior through self-directed speech. This self-directed speech takes on the function of the adult, monitoring and assisting behavior. We will discuss the concept of self-directed speech in more detail in Chapter 8.

After the child's performance is smooth and integrated, no longer needing self-directed speech to initiate behaviors, the child enters stage 3. In this stage, behavior becomes automatized and fossilized. The child no longer needs to think about the substeps and can now produce a mature performance easily, almost thoughtlessly. The link between automatization of behavior and the ZPD is not one commonly made in the Vygotskian framework, although both concepts are considered important. For example, compare the stages of learning to play a song on the piano. In the early stages, the learner has to pay attention to placement of the fingers, count the beats, and play each note carefully. The notes may not even form a melody to the learner. After much practice, the pianist will think of the melody and the notes will flow effortlessly from her fingers. Assistance from adults or others is no longer needed. The child has appropriated the skill. For most Vygotskian researchers, this is the point at which the ZPD shifts. The skill is considered to be appropriated, or acquired, and belongs to the new level of independent performance.

In the final stage, stage 4, de-automatization of performance leads to recursion though the ZPD. For Tharp and Gallimore, another stage is necessary to enhance, improve, or maintain performance. When for some reason a newly learned skill becomes de-automatized and cannot be carried out spontaneously, the child must return to other-assistance or self-assistance. Thus, teachers may find that they have to repeat already learned material even after they feel that children have attained mastery.

Tharp and Gallimore add to our understanding of the ZPD in the following ways:

1. Self-directed (private) speech is a transitional stage that facilitates independent performance.
2. Even when performance is automatized, the child may have to return to assisted performance under some conditions.

The idea of the zone of proximal development has important implications for education. It provides alternative perspectives on the way we assist children in the learning/teaching process, assess children, and define developmentally appropriate practice. In the chapters that follow we will discuss how to apply these ideas in different classroom situations.

For Further Reading

Newman D., Griffin P., & Cole, M. (1989). *The construction zone: Working for cognitive change in school.* Cambridge: Cambridge University Press.

Newman F., & Holzman L. (1993). *Lev Vygotsky: Revolutionary scientist.* New York: Routledge.

Rogoff, B., Malkin, C., & Gilbride, K. (1984). Interaction with babies as guidance in development. *New Directions for Child Development, 23,* 31–44.

Saxe, G. B., Gearhart, M., & Guberman, S. R. (1984). The social organization of early number development. *New Directions for Child Development, 23,* 19–30.

Valsiner, J. (1984). Construction of the zone of proximal development in adult-child joint action: The socialization of means. *New Directions for Child Development,   23,* 65–76.

CHAPTER 5

Developmental Accomplishments and Leading Activity: Infants and Toddlers

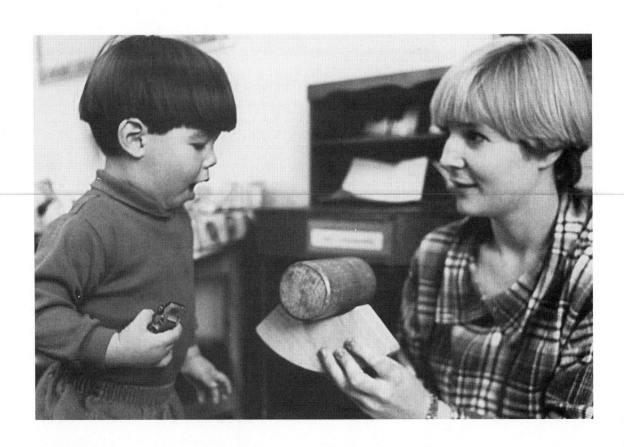

Vygotsky believed that development includes both qualitative and quantitative changes. Children go through periods of qualitative changes, when there is a change in the very nature and form of the child's mind, in the quality of thinking. Each phase heralds new cognitive and emotional structures. Likewise, there are periods when no new formations appear, but the child is still learning information. During these periods, growth occurs as a quantitative change in the number of things the child can remember and process.

We have coined the term *developmental accomplishments* to describe the new cognitive and emotional "formations" that were identified by Vygotsky and his students. Discussion of these formations is scattered in Vygotsky's writings, rather than presented as a coherent theory. After his death, colleagues and students (Leont'ev, 1977/1978; Elkonin, 1971/1977) extended and consolidated these ideas into definitive stages which are applied today in Russia.

Developmental Accomplishments

In the Vygotskian framework, developmental accomplishments are considered outgrowths of the "social situation of development" that is specific for each age (Vygotsky, 1984). The social situation of development includes both the social context and the way the child reacts to this context. Vygotsky argued that society changes its expectations and ways of treating the child as the child grows up. Therefore, the social context, or the child's social environment, is different at different ages. For example, many expectations for preschoolers are different from those for school-age children. School-age children are expected to do more for themselves; therefore, many cultures emphasize the development of deliberate behaviors in children of this age.

The social situation of development also includes the way the child interacts with this social context. As the child's abilities grow, the social context is adjusted to meet these new skills and needs. What we expect children to be able to learn and what we expect to teach them depend in part on what they are able to do. As children show they are able to do things unassisted, parents and teachers begin to demand more independence and give the child more responsibilities.

Developmental accomplishments are not the only capacities the child has but rather the ones that mature during a particular age. As certain new thinking skills and knowledge are acquired, children are also developing other skills and capacities which will come to fruition later. Thus, they are practicing for later developmental accomplishments all along. While higher mental functions do not emerge until the primary grades, children are practicing and learning to be deliberate in their mental actions during the preschool period, in memorizing a finger play during circle time, for instance. Lower mental functions are already beginning to be transformed into higher mental functions. Consequently, the idea of developmental accomplishments is not a strict stage theory in which children are seen as concentrating only on the behaviors that emerge during a particular period.

The Concept of Leading Activity

Leont'ev (1977/1978) used the concept of *leading activity* to specify the types of interactions between the child and the social environment that lead to developmental accomplishments. A leading activity is the only type of interaction that will

1. produce major developmental accomplishments
2. provide the basis for other activities (interactions)
3. induce the creation of new mental processes and the restructuring of old ones

Children engage in many types of activities, but only the leading activity is crucial for the emergence of the next developmental accomplishment. When engaged in a leading activity, the child learns skills that make it possible for him to begin the transition to other types of interactions with the environment. Leading activities shape the mind in a unique way, enabling the child to generate new mental functions and to restructure current mental functions.

Leading activities are the optimal activities for development. Although children can learn in other activities within their ZPD, leading activities are those that are most beneficial. In some cases, a child may need to return to the leading activity of the previous age if she is not able to take advantage of the one appropriate for her own age. For example, a first grader who cannot engage in learning activity can benefit from having the same behavior introduced in play, the leading activity for preschool. Toby, 6 years of age, is given a group of objects to classify. As is typical of his behavior in other learning situations, Toby does not carry out the task. Instead of sorting the objects, he builds towers and knocks them over, or he lines the objects up and plays with them. This response should indicate to the teacher that Toby may need to return to the leading activity of the previous stage and try sorting as part of a play activity. Another example is the 4-year-old child who cannot engage in play, the leading activity for preschool. This child may need to take two steps back to the activity of emotional communication with a caregiver. Once the child has interacted with the teacher and formed a bond, or one-on-one relationship, the child will then be able to begin interacting in play as she should at her age. This important personal connection must be made before the child can take advantage of playing with others.

The leading activity is different at each stage of development and varies by culture. The following leading activities have been proposed by Leont'ev (1977/1978) and Elkonin (1971/1977), specific to industrialized societies (see Table 5.1). They recognized that the leading activity is closely associated with cultural tools and specific types of cultural institutions, such as schools, designed to pass these tools to children.

The remainder of this chapter discusses the leading activities and developmental accomplishments for infancy and toddlerhood. Chapter 6 discusses the leading activities and developmental accomplishments for children in preschool, kindergarten, and the primary grades.

Table 5.1   Leading Activities by Age Group

Stage	Leading Activity	Developmental Accomplishment
Infancy	Emotional communication	Attachment, manipulation of objects, simple sensorimotor actions
Toddlerhood	Manipulation of objects	Sensorimotor thinking, emergence of self-concept
Preschool	Play	Imagination, symbolic function, and integration of emotions and thinking
Primary grades	Learning activity	Beginnings of theoretical reasoning, emergence of higher mental functions, intrinsic motivation to learn

Infancy

Leading Activity: Emotional Communication

The leading activity for infancy is *emotional communication* which for Vygotskians means the establishment of an emotional dialogue between the infant and the primary caregiver. Elkonin (1969) and Lisina (Lisina, 1974; Lisina & Galiguzova, 1980) found that this emotional dialogue evolves throughout infancy, beginning with purely emotional exchanges (e.g., smiling or cooing back and forth) and shifting to emotional dialogues over objects (e.g., smiling after shaking a rattle). Purely emotional exchanges include the parents or caregiver engaging in talking with the baby, who responds by smiling, cooing, or attending. They also include physical interactions like tickling, bouncing, or patting, with the baby responding by cooing and smiling. As the child gets older, he begins to initiate the interactions. What Elkonin and Lisina describe are the same behaviors that were called "interactional synchrony" by Tronick (1989) and others. Western psychologists have found that this type of emotional dialogue is essential for the development of the child's social and emotional life, but what Elkonin and Lisina have contributed is the idea that this dialogue also has a direct influence on cognitive development.

During the second half of the first year, the purely emotional dialogue begins to change, and the caregiver and the child hold their dialogue around objects and actions upon objects. Now the father shakes a rattle in response to the baby's smile. Around this time parents begin to label and talk about objects. Parents and others interpret the baby's actions as if the actions were communicating something. For example, 6-month-old Lisa gestures toward her teddy bear, and her sister says, "Oh, you want your bear. I'll get it for you." For infants, objects become interesting through the mediation of others. By modeling how to interact with objects and interacting with the child over the object, we provide the assistance which enables the child to acquire object manipulation. Object manipulation exists in a shared experience first, as do all other mental processes, and it is an outcome of the child's emotional dialogue with her caregiver.

Leont'ev (1977/1978) argued that emotional dialogue provides the motivation for later forms of shared activity. Because the infant communicates and wants to communicate with others, he is drawn into shared experience. Shared activity becomes a vital part of the infant's life. Vygotsky believed that during infancy all mental functions are shared, and only at the end of infancy do some of these processes become appropriated by the child. In the views of many Western psychologists, including Piaget, the end of infancy is when the "separation of self" occurs (Piaget, 1936/1952; Erikson, 1950).

In infancy, language is a tool used exclusively for strengthening emotional communication (Vygotsky, 1934/1962). The baby speaks and is spoken to as a means of communication. The link between thinking and speech is not yet established. However, speech plays a vital role in emotional communication, and without it emotional communication would not be as rich.

Developmental Accomplishments

Emotional communication is the context in which the developmental accomplishments of infancy occur. For Vygotskians these are attachment and object-oriented sensorimotor actions.

Attachment.   Although the term *attachment* was not used by Vygotskians, their concept of a fundamental emotional relationship is very similar to Western definitions of attachment (Bowlby, 1969; Bretherton, 1992). Attachment is a two-way emotional relationship, involving the active participation of both child and caregiver, and is the blueprint for future relationships the child will develop.

Many Western psychologists have studied the relationship between different types of attachment, cognitive development, and later achievement (Frankel & Bates, 1990; Grossman & Grossman, 1990). Western research links attachment to cognitive development through the child's emotional state. The unattached or poorly attached child suffers from a sense of insecurity which impairs the child's ability to learn later. The Vygotskian idea about the role of attachment in cognitive development goes beyond this. The lack of attachment also deprives the child of cognitive interactions that are necessary for mental life. Because the actual content of interactions determines the quality of shared experience, if there is no attachment, the child is deprived of important cognitive experiences. This deprivation, in turn, will influence the acquisition of mental functions. Without attachment the child cannot engage in shared activities.

Object-Oriented Sensorimotor Actions.   Emotional communication also impacts the development of *sensorimotor manipulation of objects*. By shaking the rattle, the father does not just entertain the child but models what you do with a rattle. He shows his child that a rattle can be shaken to produce a noise. He places the rattle in the baby's hands and encourages the baby to shake it. The father-child interaction over the rattle becomes a blueprint for interacting with rattles and with other objects. Shared experiences structure the child's perception, making the child focus on separate objects and their attributes. Caregivers use words like *big, small, far,* and *near* as they show the baby objects. These demonstrate and call the baby's attention to perceptual and relational characteristics.

Piaget believed that sensorimotor manipulations grow out of the baby's spontaneous body movements and actions. Babies, he felt, accidentally discover properties through random exploration (Ginsberg & Opper, 1988). Vygotsky argues that while children's manipulations are limited by their motor capabilities, the way to interact with objects is first demonstrated by others. Some evidence for the Vygotskian perspective is found in the fact that children who had been severely deprived of emotional contacts did not engage in much object manipulation even though the objects were accessible to them in the crib (Lisina, 1974; Spitz, 1946). Vygotskians argue that if object manipulation was a consequence of the baby's spontaneous actions, then object manipulation would develop independently of any social experience. The lack of attachment would not affect the child's object manipulation. However, because these emotionally deprived children also show almost a complete absence of sensorimotor manipulation, there must be a link between interacting with people and the development of exploratory behavior.

Toddlerhood

Leading Activity: Manipulation of Objects

For toddlers (age 1 to 3 years), the leading activity is the *manipulation of objects.* Through interaction with objects—touching, moving, banging, turning over—the child learns. Manipulation becomes coordinated. Instead of playing with one object at a time as infants do, toddlers play with several objects together. They put the block inside the bowl, or they stack blocks on top of each other. In contrast, infants tend to examine one block at a time, not considering how several blocks can be used together. Coordinated manipulation enables toddlers to look at relationships between objects and at their attributes. One of the relationships that toddlers discover is that one object can be used as a tool to do something to another object. This is definitely a step forward because tool use is found by experimenting and manipulation in a coordinated way.

Unlike infants, toddlers do not need other people to directly share all activities. The toddler interacts with objects when he is alone, so adults influence shared activity indirectly by the types of toys that they make available to the child for play (Elkonin, 1971/1977). Nevertheless, learning is still socially mediated.

Language is no longer a tool used just for emotional communication, as we find in infancy. For toddlers, language is intimately tied to object manipulation. It facilitates manipulation because it enables the child to retain understanding of the newly discovered attributes of objects and relationships between objects. For example, the words "put inside" will trigger a whole set of associations between an object and other objects. In addition, Vygotskians showed that the way a toddler plays with an object is determined in part by that object's name. If the caregiver hands a toddler a stick and says "spoon," the child will pretend to eat with it. If she takes a stick and pretends to eat with it, the child will mimic her and say "spoon." On the other hand, if the caregiver takes the stick and says "baby," the toddler may put the stick on the table, kiss it, and cover it with a napkin. Clearly, the physical attributes of an object are not the only things that determine the way the toddler plays with it or uses it.

Notwithstanding their use of words, toddlers do not think in words. Their words are associated with certain actions but do not form the basis of thinking. Vygotsky believed that the child associates "spoon" with eating, but does not think using the word *spoon,* as in thinking about needing a spoon to feed the baby. Words are integrated into thinking, but the child still depends on physical manipulations of objects to support problem solving. When the child can think primarily in words, then language and thinking have merged. This merger takes place during the next period, preschool.

Developmental Accomplishments

Manipulating objects leads to the following developmental accomplishments: sensorimotor thinking and self-concept.

Sensorimotor Thinking.   Like Piaget (1952), Vygotsky believed that children use *sensorimotor thinking*; that is, they solve problems using motor actions and perceptions. Unlike Piaget, Vygotsky (1934/1962) argued that sensorimotor thinking was mediated by other people through shared activity and language, and was not the result of the maturation of sensorimotor schemas, as it was in Piaget's view.

Toddlers are capable of generalizing their actions from object to object, unlike infants. They discover that some objects can be used as tools or instruments. Elkonin (1969) called this *instrumental activity.* Through the use of instruments, toddlers begin to explore the hidden attributes of objects and to separate objects from actions. These activities prepare toddlers for the transition to symbolic functioning and make it possible for the development of play in preschool.

Emerging Self-Concept.   The last major developmental accomplishment of infancy is the *emergence of self-concept,* or self-awareness (Leont'ev 1977/1978; Elkonin, 1971/1977). At this stage, toddlers become aware that they have thoughts and desires that are separate from those of their caregivers. Toddlers express this awareness by wanting to do things for themselves, asserting their own will, and acting independently from others. This independent behavior is similar to what Erikson (1950) labeled "autonomy" in children of this age. Infants participate in the emotional dialogue unaware of their separateness. Toddlers see themselves as separate entities, often having to prove it to themselves by opposing the will of others. We have all seen situations like these. Two-year-old Rick's mother tries to get him to drink a glass of milk, which he refuses to do. Finally, she says "Okay, no milk for you." He immediately reaches for the milk and tries to grab it.

Another type of activity that helps children to develop at this age is communicating with peers. Interacting and playing with other children facilitate development of language, self-concept, and sensorimotor thinking. While children at this age are not skilled in interacting with same-age mates, interaction with other children of all ages is beneficial.

For Further Reading

Elkonin, D. (1977). Toward the problem of stages in the mental development of the child. In M. Cole (Ed.), *Soviet developmental psychology*. White Plains, NY: M. E. Sharpe. (Original work published in 1959)

Leont'ev, A. (1978). *Activity, consciousness, and personality*. Englewood Cliffs, NJ: Prentice Hall. (Original work published in 1977)

CHAPTER 6

Developmental Accomplishments and Leading Activity: Preschool, Kindergarten, and Primary Grades

In this chapter, we discuss the developmental accomplishments and leading activity for preschool and kindergarten (age 2 ½ to 5) and primary grades (age 6 to 9). Ages are given for approximate orientation to the stages because individual children may have very different characteristics. Definitions of the terms *developmental accomplishments* and *leading activity* are found at the beginning of Chapter 5.

Preschool and Kindergarten

Leading Activity: Play

For Vygotskians (Leont'ev, 1977/1978; Elkonin, 1971/1977), play is the leading activity of the preschool and kindergarten period. Vygotsky and other educational theorists, such as Piaget (1945/1951), agree that play promotes development of both mental and social abilities in children. Play is both a symbolic and social activity. Details about play in the Vygotskian paradigm and the importance of play are discussed in detail in Chapter 10.

Language becomes the tool for play (Vygotsky, 1934/1962) because it enables young children to share meanings both real and invented. Through language, they can agree to pretend that a block is a glass of milk and that a piece of paper is a cookie. Language allows children to coordinate and negotiate the roles, rules, and goals of play. Zina says, "Let's pretend you are the bus driver. I'll get on the bus and buy a ticket. Then you give me money back and start driving." Without language, play would never be as rich and exciting as it is at this age.

Developmental Accomplishments

The developmental accomplishments of the preschool and kindergarten period are imagination, symbolic function, and the integration of thinking and emotions. Through play, children are able to create imaginary situations, to act as if something were a certain way. Imagination enriches the social and intellectual life and is the root of creativity. Children do more than appropriate known information, they build and recreate, developing new ideas and concepts.

Imagination.   *Imagination* is generative mental activity; it generates more ideas, different ideas. It allows children to experiment with other kinds of scenarios. For example, Joan and Tim play out the story of Little Red Riding Hood. The first time, Tim is a mean loud wolf. The second time, Joan asks him to be a nice wolf that becomes her pet instead of the mean wolf. They try this out together, changing the characteristics of the make-believe roles.

Symbolic Function.   The second developmental accomplishment is *symbolic function* (Leont'ev, 1977/1978; Elkonin, 1971/1977). Children are able to use objects, actions, words, and people to stand for something else. For example, a box can be a spaceship, moving the arms can mean "I'm flying", saying "We're aliens" makes us aliens, and pretending I'm a tree makes me a tree. To Vygotsky, this symbolic use of objects, actions, words, and people prepares the way for the learning of literacies based on the use of symbols like reading, writing, and drawing.

Children also begin to use words as concepts; this is another aspect of symbolic function. Vygotsky points out that children's first concepts are different from those of adults. Children form what he called *complexes* in which the attributes used to categorize objects are not differentiated (Vygotsky, 1962). At the beginning, attributes are tied together in one complex; the block is "big-round-red." Only after much experience both with objects and with other people, does it become "big," "round," and "red," with each attribute recognized independently. Preschool/kindergarten children may use the word *big* when they mean "big-round-red," while adults may take the child's use of the word *big* as a sign that the child's meaning is the same as it is for the adults, the one attribute "big." When asked to identify any big objects in context, young children can easily perform, but when asked to identify who is bigger in an abstract problem without the actual objects, they stumble because they cannot compare actual things.

By the end of the preschool/kindergarten period, children refine their initial complexes through interaction with people and objects. Their complexes move closer and closer to those of adults and form what Vygotsky (1934/1962) called *everyday concepts*. These everyday concepts are based on intuitions and not strict definitions, and they are not integrated into a broader structure. For example, when the child uses the word *fish,* she is referring to the object she has encountered that was labeled "fish" or a generalized idea of fishiness, including anything that swims, from goldfish to whales. She will not have in mind the strict biological definition of *fish* as a part of a scientific classification scheme.

Integration of Emotions and Thinking.   The third developmental accomplishment is the *integration of emotions and thinking* (Leont'ev, 1977/1978; Elkonin, 1971/1977; Zaporozhets & Markova, 1983). Toddlers react emotionally to immediate situations. In contrast, preschoolers and kindergarteners experience emotions in anticipation of coming situations and when remembering past experience. The preschooler or kindergartener no longer just reacts but remembers and thinks about emotions. Vygotsky described this as "emotions becoming thoughtful" (Vygotsky, 1984, p. 377).

Other Activities.   While not leading activities, other activities are beneficial for development during this period:

- Constructive activities (drama and storytelling, block building, art and drawing)
- Preacademic activities (preliteracy and premath activities)
- Motor activities (large-muscle activities)

Constructive activities, particularly when done with others, promote the same kind of shared activity as play. When children are assigned or assign themselves roles and are required to communicate with another person during and after creation, constructive activities have the same beneficial effects as play. In constructive activities like building with blocks, children learn to use different symbols than those learned during play, such as reading plans or making maps. Preacademic activities are also beneficial, but only if they emerge out of children's interests. For example, presenting these activities as a direct teaching experience, as in sitting children down and teaching all of the phonics sounds, is not appropriate. If preacademic activities are part of the child's interaction with materials, in construction or in play, then they are appropriate. Thus, writing emerges out of the desire to write messages to friends or a note to Mom or Dad. Using numbers emerges when children are trying to divide up the cups for snack time. Like the authors of such books as the *Engaging Children's Minds: The Project Approach* (Katz & Chard, 1989) or *Hundred Languages of Children* (Edwards, Gandini, & Foreman, 1994), Vygotskians argue that preacademic activities can be beneficial if they occur in context. Elkonin stresses that although preacademic activities are helpful, we should never sacrifice play, constructive activities, and movement activities for the learning of letters and numbers. We can never help a child get ready for school by stressing these skills too early in the child's development.

Motor, or movement, activities are the third type of activity that promotes development at this age. Gal'perin (1992b) and Leont'ev (1977/1978) found that motor activities that required the inhibition of reactive responses were particularly useful for the development of attention and self-regulation. They suggest that there is a relationship between motor control and later control of mental processes. For teachers, this means that children who cannot sit still and inhibit their bodies from wiggling will also have trouble attending. Thus the activities in which children are required to turn into statues or freeze would be helpful games in promoting self-regulation.

Primary Grades

Vygotsky argues that many cultures change their expectations for 6- to- 7-year-old children, who are considered ready to start formal instruction. This formal instruction almost always happens in schools, both religious and secular. All schools have a special kind of social organization and special forms of interaction (e.g., teachers work with many or several students at one time, both teachers and students interact with books). This interaction is not the same as in an apprenticeship, where one child works alongside an adult and is taught informally. Vygotskians make a distinction between formal instruction and informal instruction. They do not devalue the learning in apprenticeships but argue that the learning is different.

Formal instruction has specific characteristics that cause the mind to be shaped in a specific way. In the view of Vygotskians, all schools teach abstract thinking, so it is no accident that abstract logical thought is found primarily in societies that have schools (Gellatly, 1987; Scribner, 1977). A school can be a group of children in rural Afghanistan who are learning to read the Koran or a group of children in the United States learning to read *Cat in the Hat*. Because Vygotskians are concerned primarily with formal instruction, the leading activity for the child beginning at 6 years of age is school-related.

Leading Activity: Learning Activity

Elkonin (1971/1977) and later Davydov (1986/1988) defined the leading activity of the primary grades as learning activity. *Learning activity* is adult-guided activity around specific content that is formalized, structured, and culturally determined. Learning activity is found in schools where children begin to acquire basic literacies, such as concepts of math, science, and history, absorb images in art and literature, and use the rules of grammar. In preliterate societies, children are taught skills basic for survival, such as how to raise crops or hunt. We will consider education in its form in Western culture in this section.

In learning activity, the content is presented not as a series of interesting facts but as a discipline with its own logical structure and vocabulary. Thus, studying the ecosystem is not a learning activity unless the information is organized to teach the vocabulary and classification system of that science or its scientific concepts.

Scientific concepts are built upon the everyday concepts acquired through experience and intuitive thinking. Scientific concepts, however, require another way of thinking; they are based on a logical hierarchy. Children will not understand concepts such as "volume" if they do not have everyday concepts of "liquids" and "measuring." The scientific concept directly depends on the child's everyday understandings of the world. As children learn scientific concepts, the meaning of liquids and measuring changes. It is a two way process; scientific and everyday concepts grow into one another. The scientific concept is modified by the everyday concept, and the everyday concept is changed by the learning of the scientific concept.

In the primary grades, language is the fundamental means of transmission of content and processes in learning activity. In their definition of language, Vygotskians include not only the spoken word but also reading, writing, and graphical representations (drawings). Children engage in learning activity by talking with the teacher or other students and by reading texts and writing their own interpretations. Language enables children to reflect on their inner thought processes and makes a major contribution to the emergence of higher mental functions. Language in all its forms is the currency of exchange in the classroom and the vehicle for introducing the literacies of society and allowing children to master them. For example, spoken and written language facilitates the learning of the languages of math or art.

Developmental Accomplishments

In mastering content, children attain the developmental accomplishments of this period: the beginnings of theoretical reasoning, the emergence of higher mental functions, and the development of intrinsic motivation (Elkonin, 1971/1977; Davydov, 1988; Kozulin & Presseisen, 1995).

Beginnings of Theoretical Reasoning.   The term *theoretical reasoning* describes the way that children think about the content of the learning activity, the concepts of math, science, and history, for example. When reasoning theoretically, children operate on the essential properties of objects or ideas which may or may not be perceptually visible or intuitively obvious. The essential property has been identified by that scientific discipline and is not necessarily a product of everyday experience. For example, children lacking theoretical reasoning would place dolphins in the fish category because they both swim and live in the water. Children with theoretical reasoning would use properties such as having live young, lactating, and being warm-blooded to place a dolphin in the mammal category. Scientific concepts are taught and presented within a conceptual system that enables children to use ideas that they cannot see or that are not intuitively apparent. The idea of "mammal" has meaning because it is part of the taxonomy of kingdom, phylum, class, order, family, genus, and species. Only learning activities teach these scientific concepts (e.g., Karpov & Bransford, 1995).

Vygotskians believe that children 6 to 10 years of age are beginning to acquire theoretical reasoning, but the process is not completed until age 18 or even later. However, the primary grades are formative years for the development of basic literacies about the units, or concepts, of the content area that will facilitate theoretical reasoning. For example, the basic unit in math is number, so learning about the properties of number facilitates the acquisition of later theoretical reasoning about math. Vygotskians believe that primary grade teachers should not hesitate to make the underlying scientific concepts explicit. So when the word *mammal* is used, teachers should take the time to give the definition of *mammal* and to explain that it is a way of categorizing animals, and part of the *taxonomy* used in biology. Another example is the idea that "form follows function," which is one of the underlying principles of science and technology. Children learn that form follows function when they study different kinds of houses that are built for different environmental conditions (e.g., igloos, tepees) or different kinds of vehicles designed to carry different loads (e.g., trucks, automobiles)

Emergence of Higher Mental Functions.   The second developmental accomplishment is the *emergence of higher mental functions*. When learning activity is organized according to the principles listed above, Davydov (1986) found that planning, monitoring, and evaluating of thinking, and deliberate memory were also developed. Gal'perin (1969) found that focused attention is developed through learning activity as well. Children begin to recognize appropriate and inappropriate strategies in problem solving because they notice which properties of their action were relevant and irrelevant to the completion of a task. For example, they know that to measure something the ruler must be placed in an exact way and you must read a specific number. They discover that the specific size of the ruler is not relevant. After numerous interactions with rulers, they begin to identify the appropriate strategy for measuring something that is longer than their ruler.

Davydov (1986) also asked second graders to classify math problems after solving them. He found that children classified the problems based on the type of arithmetic operation, such as addition or subtraction, and not on the similar numbers used in the problems. This ability to identify what is relevant emerged, but only after children had had experience with many math problems presented in learning activity.

In the early primary grades, higher mental functions are just emerging, so children are able to perform some strategies but need contextual support or assistance to use them effectively, such as shared activities with peers or the teacher. Because planning, monitoring, and evaluating thinking are just beginning, children may not be fully aware of their own thinking, and they will require shared activity to perform at the higher level of their ZPD. Children will need support in the form of *external mediators,* or visible external reminders, to initiate deliberate memory or other types of shared activity to help them to reflect on their own thinking (see Chapters 7 and 9). Verbal reminders made by the teacher, a peer, or the child himself are also useful. Writing and drawing provide additional support for reflective thought. Continued experience in learning activity will strengthen and nurture the further development of higher mental functions throughout the child's school years.

Intrinsic Motivation.   The final developmental accomplishment of this period is *intrinsic motivation.* By engaging in learning activity, children become interested in learning for its own sake. Instead of learning to please others, or learning as a by-product of play, or learning to keep social relationships going, learning becomes an end in itself. Davydov (1986) contrasts children who acquired intrinsic motivation through learning activity with those who did not. Children with intrinsic motivation had a pervasive curiosity and intensity of purpose which they applied to many areas, and not only those introduced by adults. They were interested in and began to pursue study without being requested to do so. When asked to study something, they found something to make themselves interested. The children have what is called *nonpragmatic curiosity,* interest that exists even though there may be no tangible payoff. Children without intrinsic motivation, Davydov notes, were primarily motivated by grades or by praise from the teacher.

For Vygotskians, lack of intrinsic motivation is caused by the interaction between the child and the social context. Either the social context does not support or value learning, or the child cannot yet differentiate between learning and play. The social context must convey a set of expectations relevant to the essence of the learning activity. For example, teachers must let the child know that not just any product is good enough but only those products that meet certain standards. Katie solves 10 addition problems, but only 2 are correct. The teacher must point out the incorrect ones, providing assistance so Katie can answer those correctly. If the teacher just says "Good job!" she is not supporting expectations that will lead to Katie's interest in learning. On the other hand, if a child cannot distinguish between play and learning, she will lose interest in trying to learn when things are not fun and exciting. Thus you cannot take a bright 4-year-old and use learning activity as the leading activity. A 4-year-old is not developmentally ready to make the transition between play and learning. Only when both components—the social context and the child's abilities—are appropriate will learning activity lead to intrinsic motivation.

Optimizing Learning/Teaching in the Classroom

One of the ways to promote the development of learning activity was proposed by Gal'perin (1959/1969). He called his approach "errorless learning." This approach has some very specific characteristics that go beyond the scope of this book. However, several useful recommendations can be drawn from Gal'perin's work.

Natural Errors

Vygotskians recognize that there are different kinds of errors. Only some of them require intervention, while others are natural or even beneficial. When errors occur for a short period of time and then are outgrown, they are a natural part of the learning process. Some examples are invented spelling, using stick figures in drawing, and reversing letters. Some errors are beneficial in the learning process in providing feedback to the child about her performance. By correcting these errors the child can improve her performance. When a child reads the word *hat* as *hit* and the sentence no longer makes sense, the error makes the child look at the word and try to read it correctly. The child is able to think about the error and the reason for it. This type of error creates cognitive dissonance and may even trigger the child's curiosity.

On the other hand, some errors are not beneficial. These are errors that the child does not understand or cannot seem to correct even after feedback from the teacher or support from the social context. In some children, natural errors, such as reversing letters, do not disappear in a reasonable amount of time and consequently become a problem. An example would be a third grader who is still reversing and confusing *b* and *d*. Such errors are extremely frustrating and can have a negative effect on the child's motivation to learn. These *repeated errors* are very resistant to change and become a major problem in the classroom.

Automatization of Mental Actions

Gal'perin believed that before any new concept, skill, or strategy is internalized, it exists for a period of time in an externally supported form. It can be observed in the child's overt verbalizations or the way she manipulates objects. It is during this time that the teacher has access to the skill and can guide development of the skill by modifying external support for it. Once the skill is internalized, it becomes *automatized* and *folded,* which means that it is not easily accessible to correction. The child may even be unaware of the strategy or concept in an explicit way. When automatized, the entire behavior is automatically activated, so the teacher cannot stop it at the right moment to correct a missing or defective part. For example, consider an adult who turns left when exiting a parking lot to go home but really needs to turn right to go to the store. The left-turn habit is so strong that the entire behavior cannot be broken into parts. The driver may not even notice that he has made a wrong turn until he is on his way home instead of heading to the store.

Automatization explains why it is difficult to correct some things we have learned initially incorrectly but cannot seem to correct even though we know we are wrong. Some examples are incorrect spellings, mispronunciation of certain words, and incorrect math facts. In all these cases, we recognize the mistake after we have repeated it and wish we could have stopped ourselves beforehand.

The traditional way of correcting this kind of mistake is to point out the error after it has been committed. As most teachers can tell you, pointing out the error afterward has very little effect on error production the next time.

Preventing and Correcting Repeated Errors

Gal'perin (1959/1969) designed his method of *errorless learning* to help teachers prevent repeated errors and help children correct them. First, he encouraged teachers to keep in mind the past mistakes of students when planning learning experiences. For example, if you know that children confuse the colors orange and red, when you present those colors, you point out right away that they are different. Or when you show the letters *b* and *d,* you point out the ways in which they are different. As children write these letters, encourage them to analyze their own *b*s and *d*s for the elements the teacher has emphasized. Thus the teacher anticipates the elements that will be confusing.

Gal'perin points out that teachers should not leave the discovery of the essential elements to the children. He did not believe that trial-and-error learning was beneficial in the school context. In school, learning by trial and error leads to repeated errors and is very frustrating because the child cannot guess what the teacher is getting at.

Once the teacher has explained all of the necessary elements, he has to monitor the process of acquisition, provide various kinds of assistance, such as shared experiences and external mediators, and encourage the use of private speech. The teacher must make sure that the child's understanding reflects all the essential components and that the child can apply the knowledge or skill to new problems without distorting the information. A typical error for second graders is to misuse capitalization. To use the idea of errorless learning, the teacher generates with the children a list of all of the situations in which capitals are used. These are placed on a card on each child's desk (external mediator). Children who work on an assignment to practice capitalization use private speech and the external mediator. As they go down a list of words, they ask themselves at each word, "Should this be capitalized?" After several practice sentences children discuss their results with a partner, and then the teacher comes by to monitor their progress. In a few weeks most children will not need the card at their desks and will not use private speech. Some children may still require external support for a while longer.

When repeated errors appear, according to Gal'perin, it is necessary to go back and see what caused the misunderstanding. Were all of the essential elements explicitly conveyed to the child, or did the child miss one of these? Did the child have enough practice, or was independent performance encouraged before the child was ready? Was enough support offered to the child to enable the child to master all of the pieces of the skill or concept?

Once the cause is found, the teacher must compensate for the missing experience or help the child relearn the information. For example, the child may be missing a rule that will help him clear up the misunderstanding. In some cases, the child will need more practice with the missing rule being emphasized or even visually highlighted, say, with a different colored pen.

We have found Gal'perin's work particularly helpful in the correction of repeated mistakes or automatized mistakes. He suggests that some external mediator be devised to signal the specific error. For example, if a child is misreading a specific consonant combination, the teacher writes it in a different color to focus attention on it. The child can also underline the text by himself or a peer can do it. When the child reaches these letters in the text, the teacher encourages him to stop and notice that it is different. Having the child "stop" blocks the initiation of the repeated error. For a while, the child will need the external mediator, but if he practices enough times correctly, the new, corrected skill will become automatized, replacing the incorrect one. It is important that the child stop *before* the error; correcting afterwards will not help.

Generally speaking, the idea of correcting repeated errors can also be applied to areas other than academics. We have used this technique to help several children correct their inappropriate behavior; these included a child who hit others, a child who used inappropriate language, and a child who interrupted the teacher constantly.

For Further Reading

Davydov, V. V., & Markova, A. K. (1983). A concept of educational activity for school children. *Journal of Soviet Psychology, 21*(2), 50–76. (Original work published in 1981)

Davydov, V. V. (Ed.). (1991). *Psychological abilities of primary school children in learning mathematics*. Vol. 6, *Soviet studies in mathematics education*. Reston, VA: National Council of Teachers of Mathematics.

Gal'perin, P. Y. (1992b). The problem of attention. *Journal of Russian and East European Psychology, 30*(4), 83–91. (Original work published in Russian in 1976)

Karpov, Y. V. & Bransford, J. D. (1995). L. S. Vygotsky and the doctrine of empirical and theoretical learning. *Educational Psychologist, 30*(2), 61-66.

Kozulin, A. (1984). *Psychology in Utopia: Toward a social history of Soviet psychology*. Cambridge, MA: MIT Press.

Kozulin, A., & Presseisen, B. Z. (1995). Mediated learning experience and psychological tools: Vygotsky's and Feuerstein's perspectives in a study of student learning. *Educational Psychologist, 30*(2), 67-76.

Van der Veer, R., & Valsiner, J. (1991). *Understanding Vygotsky: A quest for synthesis*. Oxford: Blackwell.

Tactics for Promoting Development and Learning/Teaching

In this section we discuss several different tactics teachers can use in the classroom. These tactics have been used in Russian classrooms and pilot-tested in the United States. Teachers can use these tactics to improve the contextual support they give to the child's learning, but to use them properly they must keep in mind the child's zone of proximal development and the leading activity and developmental accomplishments of the child's age level. In addition, these tactics provide teachers with another way of looking at the learning/teaching process. In practice, the various tactics are intertwined, but for the purpose of fully understanding each tactic, we discuss them as separate entities here. The tactics are organized under three general headings—mediators, language, and shared activities—and are described in the following chapters:

CHAPTER 7

Tactics: Using Mediators

Teachers can promote development and help children move from assisted to independent performance. The Vygotskian paradigm suggests that one way to do this is to create mediators that children can use as tools. Mediators facilitate the handing over of responsibility to the child. Developed with adult assistance, they can be used by the child without the teacher's physical presence. In this chapter we describe mediators and suggest ways in which they can be used in an early childhood classroom.

The Function of Mediators

In Vygotsky's work, a *mediator* is something that stands as an intermediary between an environmental stimulus and an individual response to that stimulus (See Chapter 3, Figure 3.1). A mediator facilitates the child's development by making it easier for the child to perform a certain behavior. In the Vygotskian framework, mediators become mental tools when the child incorporates them into his own activity. Like other cultural tools, mediators exist first in shared activity and then are appropriated by the child. When Linda is learning how to read, the teacher says, "Look at the first letter. What sound does it make?" Linda thinks to herself, "Look at the first letter," and this internal speech acts as a mediator to facilitate reading. Tony is learning to add numbers. He uses his fingers to help him calculate. His fingers act as a mediator, making his adding more accurate. In each case, the child uses the mediator to expedite behavior.

Vygotsky believed that adults possess complex, abstract mediators to help them think. Some of the mediators adults use include words, symbols, graphic models, plans, and maps. These mediators may be visible to others, such as a list of things to do, or they may be internal. Adults use these mediators naturally, in an integrated fashion, and often automatically, without consciously thinking about it.

Sometimes adults are faced with situations in which the automatic use of mediators is interrupted or made difficult in some way. In such situations, adults resort to using external overt mediators instead of their internal ones. For example, an adult who is using an unfamiliar stove must look at the dials on the control panel (the external mediator) and figure out which burner is which. When using a familiar stove, the adult has an internal pattern relating the burners to the dials. Another example is an adult who is driving a car with a shifting pattern that is new. The adult will look at the diagram on the handle of the gear shift to make sure that she is in first gear and not in reverse!

Sometimes children will forget the behavior they learned through external mediation and need to use the mediator once again for a short time. For children mediators are external and overt and are not necessarily integrated into their thought patterns. External, overt mediators are visible to others and the child and can even be tangible. For example, Mr. Wong wants the children to remember to speak in soft voices during group meeting time. He puts a small stuffed mouse on his desk right before the transition to group meeting time. The stuffed mouse is a tangible mediator, reminding the children to speak with lowered voices. The children may require practice in using the mediator and prompting by an adult because they may not remember on their own. To make the mouse into a mediator, Mr. Wong has the children practice being quiet when the mouse is out and being noisy when he hides it behind his back. He asks the children to tell him what the mouse means. He even prompts the children to whisper to themselves, "When the mouse is out, I am quiet as a mouse."

External Mediators as Scaffolding

Overt mediators function as scaffolding, helping the child make the transition from maximum assisted performance to independent performance. The goal is to remove or to stop using the external mediators once the child has internalized their meaning. External mediators are a *temporary step* designed to lead the child to independence. Teachers plan the type of mediator to be used as well as how the external mediator will be removed as the child gains independence and appropriates the behavior and the tool. The appropriate time for removing the mediator cannot be determined exactly. Sometimes children will forget the external mediator and need to use it again for a short time. Sometimes a few successes are enough, and you can begin weaning the child from the overt mediator very quickly.

Types of Mediators

Mediators can be verbal, visual, or physical. Speech and written words are verbal mediators. A simple behavior, such as learning how to knit, can be mediated by the words *knit* and *purl.* These words can be said aloud, as in "knit, knit, purl, purl," to facilitate creating a certain pattern of stitches. A mediator can also be materialized, or tangible. Pictures or diagrams are examples of visual mediators. For example, an adult might use a picture of the stitch pattern as a reminder of what to do. A physical mediator is a set of behaviors, such as a *habit* or *ritual,* that triggers a mental process. For example, a finger play or clapping pattern can mediate behaviors for coming to group meeting time, helping children to remember to sit in a circle and look at the teacher.

Verbal, visual, and physical mediators can affect the processing of complex information, such as classification. In some cases, words describing the categories act as verbal mediators. When Louella is sorting blocks, the teacher gives her the words *small, medium,* and *large* as verbal mediators for sorting. The child says these words to herself as she sorts. The teacher could also give her a visual mediator, such as a small circle, a medium-size circle, and a large circle (see Figure 7.1).

Unlike adults, who primarily use internal, verbal mediators to direct mental processes and behaviors, children need something more concrete and tangible. Ms. Martinez wants to limit the number of children who participate in the block-building area. To provide a tangible mediator, she cuts out pictures of four chairs and

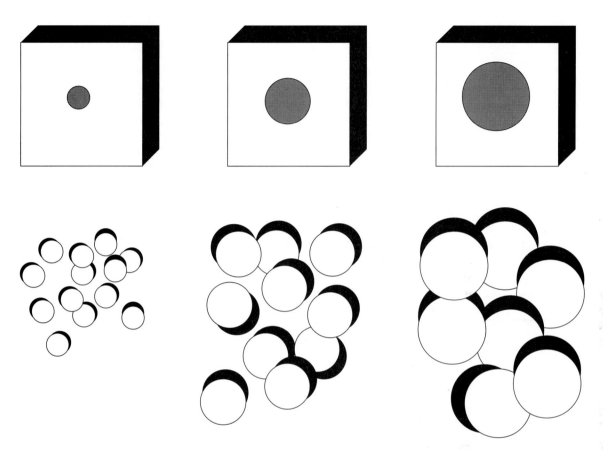

Figure 7.1.   Boxes with external mediators for sorting

places the pictures in a box at the entrance of the block area. When Michael enters the block area, he takes a chair picture and puts it in a pocket next to the box. When all of the chair pictures are gone, it signals that a new child cannot enter. A less effective strategy would be to rely on the children themselves to remember that only four can enter the area because some of the children cannot count meaningfully or use counting as a way to regulate their actions. By providing the chair pictures, Ms. Martinez provides a tangible mediator to help the children to remember the limit.

As children gain more experience, they independently initiate the use of mediators. The first attempts to invent mediators may take the form of such statements as "I can only read when I sit on the beanbag chair" or "I need my magic pen to write." Adults often take such statements as examples of flights of fantasy, but Vygotsky would say that these statements mark the beginning of using external mediation, that is, using objects to mediate mental processes. The mediators chosen may or may not be the same ones that are used by adults. As long as the child assigns his own personal meaning to the mediator and uses it to guide behavior, the mediator will be useful.

Mediation of Social and Emotional Behaviors

Vygotsky points out that external mediators are often used to regulate social interactions. Adults toss a coin or draw straws to decide an issue, such as who will do the chores. Children use rhymes or finger plays ("one potato, two potato"; "scissors, paper, stone") to settle arguments about who goes first or how long each child has a toy. Some external mediators are passed from one generation of children to another in the playgrounds of the world. Without older children around, it is unlikely that preschool children would know about these things. In some cases, teachers may have to give children the external mediators that they would otherwise get from older children.

People also use external mediators to control their emotions. They count to 10 before reacting, as a way to check their anger or fear. Children chant rhymes like "Sticks and stones may break my bones, but words will never hurt me" instead of hitting. People also use mediators when making up after an argument. Rituals such as shaking hands or apologizing are used to end arguments and reestablish social relationships. The rules of a game are another common mediator (see Chapter 10) used to regulate social and emotional behavior. Adults may need to supply children with these mediators. For example, a teacher may demonstrate counting to ten or taking 10 deep breaths to help a child overcome her angry feelings. A parent may use "monster spray" (a spray bottle of water) to allay a child's bedtime fears. Supplying a child's special blanket can help him calm down and fall asleep at nap time. All of these external mediators help children to control and regulate their emotions.

Arguments are a common problem among preschool children. In one classroom, peace bracelets are used for two boys who often get into aggressive arguments with each other, primarily during outdoor playtime. Before they go outside on the playground, Ms. Schram gives Ian and Jason each a peace bracelet to wear. She has the boys put the bracelets on after all of the other children have gone outside. At the same time, she has them say aloud what they will do: "These bracelets will help us remember to solve our disagreements with words. We won't hit each other. If we need help, we go to the teacher." After each boy has repeated the meaning of the mediator, she lets them go outside and checks in 5 minutes to see if they are fighting. She repeats this procedure each day. At the end of a week, she finds that most of the time they make it through the first 10 minutes without any disagreements. When she comes by, they both point to their bracelets to signal that they remember. In 2 weeks, she leaves them alone to put on the bracelets and remind themselves about their meaning. Three weeks later, she no longer requires them to use the bracelets at all.

Sharing is another typical behavior that causes problems in preschool. External mediation can also help children to remember to share. In Mr. Gleason's classroom, Sally has a hard time remembering to share with other children, especially when she is at a learning center or involved in a small-group activity. Mr. Gleason uses sharing clothespins that are bright pink. When the children arrive in the center, he has them each clip one on to their clothes. "These pins," he says, "will help you remember that everyone gets the same amount." He then demonstrates what the same amount is using two teddy bears. "Is this the same amount?" he asks as he puts 2 chips in front of one bear and 10 in front of another. "No!" the children say loudly. "Is this the same amount?" he says as he puts 4 in front of one bear and 4 in front of the other. "Yes!" they respond. Then he gives the box of chips to Sally. "Sally, you make sure everyone has the same amount." Sally now gives each child a chip until everyone has 4. The next time there is an activity where it is important for sharing to occur, Mr. Gleason brings out the sharing clothespins and prompts the appropriate speech, making sure that Sally gets practice being in charge of sharing every other day. By the end of the second week, Sally is the first one saying "Everyone gets the same amount." She no longer hoards the pencils, chips, or paper from other children.

External Mediation of Cognition

The idea of using mediation to amplify and support cognitive development has been applied in a variety of classrooms in Russia and in the United States. In early childhood education, mediators are most useful in assisting children within their ZPD in the areas of perception, attention, memory, thinking, and self-regulation.

Perception

Leonid Venger, one of Vygotsky's followers, suggests that children learn perceptual categories through external mediation (Venger, 1969/1977, 1986; Zaporozhets, 1959/1977). Everyday objects become sensory standards that help children perceive differences in color, size, shape, and even sound. For example, children learn the difference between orange and red when they compare an orange to a tomato. If two year olds are just given color cards with no contextual clues and then asked which is red and which is orange, they may have a hard time answering. When the everyday object is included as a contextual clue, toddlers answer at a much higher level. Asking "Is it the color of a tomato or the color of an orange?" will elicit more correct answers. Venger argues that exposure to everyday objects in which the perceptual characteristics are identified helps in the development of perceptual categories.

Attention

Children use mediators to attend to, or focus on, objects, events, and behaviors. Vygotskians are interested in deliberate attention, when the child consciously focuses his mind. This higher mental function is different from the spontaneous attention that children display for bright-colored objects, loud noises, and perceptually distinctive events. The ability to attend deliberately is a necessary skill for learning because the thing that is most attention-grabbing may not be the most important characteristic of what the child is learning about. Children have to learn to ignore competing or distracting information and focus on specific characteristics that are important to solving a problem or learning a task. In reading, it may not be important that the letter *b* is red, but the orientation of the letter—which side of the line has the bulge—is critical.

In a typical early childhood classroom, children are asked to attend to specific behaviors and simultaneously to ignore distractions. Sometimes they are not even asked to attend but are expected to know what to attend to and how to attend. Adults, knowing how to focus their attention, may become adult-centric and forget what confuses children. For example, when Mr. Surijan calls the children to group time, he expects them to come quickly, find a place to sit, stay seated, look at the teacher, and ignore the person they were playing with just a moment before. Without realizing it Mr. Surijan is asking children to attend to an entirely new set of cues, a difficult task for many of them.

Vygotskians argue that young children cannot attend deliberately without contextual support from mediators (Leont'ev, 1932/1994). The mediator must remind the child of the need to concentrate and ignore the distractions of other children, pictures on the wall, or interesting toys around the room. In the example above, Mr. Surijan did not give very strong cues or mediators to help the children to attend. Sitting in a circle may not be an effective mediator for attention since children may sit in a circle at other times. Children need a more obvious, tangible mediator that is used only at group time, such as a stuffed animal or puppet that only appears at group time, a hat that the teacher wears to signal group time, a special song or rhyme to begin the meeting, or a special carpet square to sit on only during that time. Some children may need more mediators than others. Spencer and Jacob have no trouble coming to group time and settling down. Mauricia and Bernie need all of the mediators Mr. Surijan can invent!

Children in first and second grade need to learn to monitor their own attention. They need to become aware of what they are supposed to attend to and when they are losing their concentration. Teachers must help children label what is most important and distinguish it from irrelevant features. They can use gestures such as pointing, coloring, highlighting, or underlining to draw the child's attention to something. For example, a child who is having trouble remembering to read the last part of a word can be helped by having that part of the word highlighted. Children can also do this highlighting for themselves.

Memory

Another higher mental function that can be assisted through mediation is deliberate memory. Most teachers and parents say that young children have very good memories sometimes. Because their memory processes tend to be reactive, young children easily recall a catchy song or a bright, colorful picture. The difficulty comes when we ask them to remember something that is not visually distinctive or of particular interest to them.

Psychologists believe that young children remember reactively because they lack both the strategies for remembering and the metacognitive skills necessary for monitoring the memory process (Gage & Berliner, 1992). Many Western psychological theories identify the skills that children lack, but few describe how to develop these skills. Most of the memory strategies discussed in the research are meant to improve an already developed, organized memory; they seem to be less effective with young children. For example, the "method of loci" strategy is a difficult memory strategy for a young child but is effective for adults who already have a base of memories. When you use the method of loci, you imagine a place you know well and then form an image of each object to be remembered in a particular spot or room in that place. For example, you might associate mental images of what you want to buy at the store with different rooms in your house—bread in the hall, milk in the kitchen, and so on. Young children could not even systematically remember the rooms, let alone make visual associations with each room.

Vygotsky believed that the child's selective memory is due to the lack of intentional control of the memory process rather than the absence of specific strategies for remembering (Vygotsky, 1978, 1983). The problem is not that children cannot remember anything, but that they cannot retain and retrieve the right information at the right time. When required to remember in a deliberate way, they may have trouble.

Intentional control of memory becomes more and more necessary as the child approaches school age because we begin to expect children to remember by themselves. In preschool we remind children constantly, but in first and second grade, children are expected to take responsibility for their own memory. The teacher gives the child information and it is up to her to remember it independently. The child must provide the organization and practice strategies necessary for recall as well as activate the memory at the right time. For example, by second grade, children must remember to take things back and forth from home to school, whether it is homework, a note from the teacher, shoes for gym, or a snack to contribute to a classroom activity. For some children the transition between dependence on adult prompts to remembering without help is easy, but for others it is a painful process. Some only remember what they were supposed to bring at the moment they walk into the classroom! In other cases, memory is triggered when the child sees the teacher. Teachers and parents may find themselves punishing these children for forgetting. They are often hard pressed to find positive ways to get them to remember.

In first and second grade, teachers typically give many directions to children orally without mediational support to help them remember what to do. Ms. Margolis expects her children to remember that there are three centers that they must visit during center learning time. Many of the children have no trouble remembering, but Ida, Joseph, and Dionnia never get past the first center. No matter what Ms. Margolis does, these three children go through parts of the first center and then become wanderers around the room. Ms. Margolis decides to give them an external mediator in the form of a ticket with the numbers 1, 2, and 3 written on it. After she sends the other children to the centers, she sits down with her wandering threesome and has them write down in their own way something that will remind them of the centers they are supposed to go to. Ida scribbles after each number, Joseph writes letters, and Dionnia draws a picture. Ms. Margolis pins the notes to their clothes with a clothespin. "When you have finished at the center," she tells them, "check it off on your ticket. Then the ticket will help you remember where to go next." By the end of the first week, only Ida and Dionnia need to use the tickets. By the end of the third week, all three children have begun to remember the routine.

As with perception and attention, Vygotskians propose using external mediators to provide scaffolding for the development of deliberate memory. External mediation is an intermediary step, enabling the child to act more independently than if the adult tells the child what to do, while providing some assistance. External mediators include a child-produced list of things to do, a sticker on the paper to remind the child to write his name on it, a picture poster of how we remember, or a ring to remember where to place your fingers on a pencil. All of these encourage the use of memory strategies and promote retrieval. These mediators help the child to initiate the correct action at the right time.

Using external mediators to initiate memory is not a new idea; in fact, adults use them all of the time. We make lists of things to do, use calendars, and have beepers. Many time-management techniques incorporate clever external mediators to help us stay on task and on target. What is different in the Vygotskian framework is the idea that mediators are tools of the mind that can and must be taught to children, beginning as young as 3 and 4 years of age. For obvious reasons, these techniques should be introduced in an age-appropriate manner early in school, instead of waiting until a study skills class in high school.

External mediators are also advantageous because they can be used in situations when the teacher is not present. They remind the child before it is too late. So much of the time, we remind children after the fact about what they should have remembered because we are not present to remind them beforehand. Alex knows that he should use words and not grab toys. In fact, after he has grabbed toys from other children, he admits that he should have used words. However, in the heat of the moment he forgets the appropriate social strategy. Coaching him after the incident has limited effect. If the teacher could follow him around and remind him at the appropriate time, he would not forget, but this, of course, is not practical. To assist Alex's memory, his teacher uses Gregory, a small stuffed animal that Alex wears on his wrist (of the hand he grabs with) as a mediator. The mediator is there to remind him to "use words and not grab." Alex practices what he will say and do when he is wearing Gregory. Wearing Gregory on his arm seems to be enough to initiate the appropriate strategy. When he is wearing Gregory, Alex succeeds in talking instead of grabbing. Gregory helps Alex to remember to use words when the teacher is not around to remind him. With enough practice at using words and experiencing successful outcomes to social interactions, Alex no longer needs Gregory because he has internalized what to do.

Thinking

External mediation can facilitate the development of thinking and reasoning. Mediators help children to monitor and reflect on their own thinking and prompt metacognitive skills.

Any abstract relationship can be presented with materialized models: graphs, pictures, manipulatives, objectives, and drawings. In the typical early childhood classroom, we do use mediators to model many conceptual relationships, such as number relationships, classification, seriation, and patterns. Ms. Pierce asks Joey to put four pictures into a series to show what comes first, second, third, and fourth. Joey picks up a picture and puts it on the table. He becomes confused with the second picture. Ms. Pierce puts an arrow on the table pointing from left to right with the numbers 1, 2, 3, and 4 written on it. With the mediator of the numbered line, Joey is able to put the pictures in order (see Figure 7.2).

Figure 7.2.   Sequencing pictures using an external mediator

Venger (1969/1977, 1986) proposes that many types of relationships can be taught using mediators. These relationships include social roles, musical patterns, sound-letter correspondences, the elements of stories (story grammar), union and intersection of sets, projections of three-dimensional objects into two dimensional space, speed and distance, and money value.

Mediators such as a Venn diagram can illustrate how two categories of objects are similar and different. Two circles that completely overlap represent the idea that the categories are the same. Two distinct circles represent the idea that the categories have no characteristics in common. When the two circles partially overlap, it means that some characteristics are shared and some are not (see Figure 7.3). By using this visual mediator, children are able to classify objects at a much more abstract level than if they are merely asked to put the objects into piles. This mediator can be used first for real objects and then for ideas, as in asking second graders how two stories are the same or different (see Figure 7.4).

Some teachers use word maps or concept webs to help children see the relationship between different concepts, ideas, or words (see Figure 7.5). In a web major categories can be written in larger print than subcategories. Developing the web as the children contribute ideas helps to crystallize and sharpen their understanding of the relationships.

The use of graphical representations is also promoted in the Vygotskian paradigm (Brofman, 1991; Venger, 1969/1977, 1986). Children are encouraged to draw and redraw their conception about how things look or work. They move back and forth between the real object and their graphic representation, modifying it as they

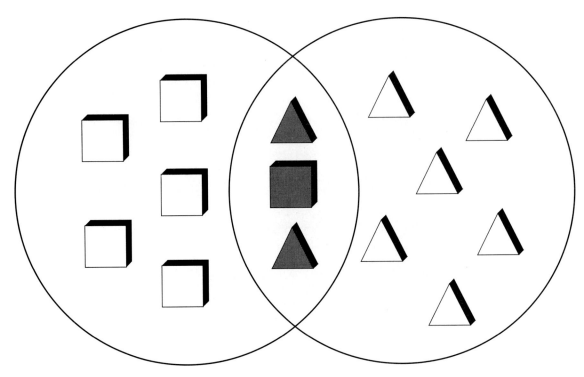

Figure 7.3.   Example of Venn diagrams used for sorting

notice more or understand more. The drawing captures what they understand so they can look at it and see if it matches what they see when they return to look at the object. This idea has been used by the educators in northern Italy with great success (Edwards, Gandini, & Foreman, 1994). For example, in a study of snow, children drew different states of water and then experimented with real snow. Based on their observations and discoveries, the children redrew and reconceptualized their understandings, and their understandings deepened and grew more complex. For example, look at the following drawing of a child's understanding of how to bake cookies (Figure 7.6). As Jeremy drew the picture, he discussed what happened at each step. In drawing the process, he became aware that some steps had to come first. His understanding of the process changed from a global one of cookie baking, to a formula or recipe with specific actions to be taken at each step along the way.

Self-Regulation

One of the goals of the Vygotskian approach is to develop self-regulation of cognitive processes. Children should develop the ability to monitor, evaluate, and regulate their own thinking processes. This ability begins to emerge in first and second grade, but the foundation for it is laid in preschool. External mediators play a big role in helping children make the transition from being regulated by adults to being self-regulated. They provide the scaffolding necessary for semi-independent regulation.

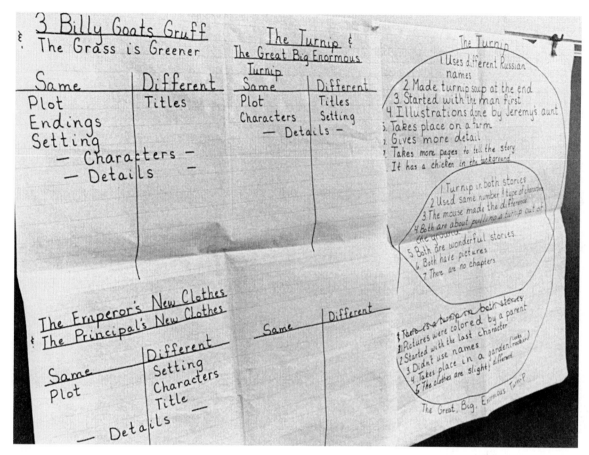

Figure 7.4. Using a Venn diagram as a mediator for story analysis

A written daily schedule for the children to look at and refer to is one external mediator that teachers often use in classrooms. To make the mediator more helpful, include a clock face marked with the approximate times for doing things on the schedule. Next to the schedule place a clock so that the children see what time it is and refer back and forth between the marked clock face and the clock. Use the schedule during the day to discuss what to do next. Soon you will find that the children utilize the schedule too, even though they may not know how to read.

Use external mediators such as songs, rhymes, or a timer to signal activities that have a short duration, such as cleanup time or other transitions. Make sure the song or rhyme is long enough so that when it is finished, the children have finished the activity and are ready for the next thing. If you use a timer, make sure it visibly shows how much time is left. Digital timers do not usually work well, but an analog timer with a dial or a three-minute egg timer in the shape of an old-fashioned hour glass is useful. For a preschool child, the idea of being ready for the next activity in

Figure 7.5.   Using a word map as an external mediator

3 minutes makes no sense. Three minutes may seem like a lifetime or a moment, depending on what the child is doing. Children need an external reminder to help them tell when the time is coming to an end. Thus, a song with a predictable melody and ending will signal "I have one song's worth of time to finish," and they will be better able to gauge how fast to move than with just a verbal reminder.

Older children are able to invent their own mediators and use lists and menus to regulate their own behavior. One teacher in a mixed-age class (K–2) uses menus for reading and language arts and for math. The menu reminds the child of what she is supposed to do during reading time (see Figure 7.7). At the beginning of the year, the teacher and the child fill in the plan together. By the end of the year, the child fills in more and more of the plan himself. Each week this teacher also asks the children a reflection question designed to get them to think about their own mental processes. This has been helpful in producing more self-regulatory behavior. Once when the teacher was late coming in from recess, she was shocked to see the entire class, including the kindergartners, fast at work without her. They had taken out their menus and were working furiously at their tasks unprompted. The room was hushed except for several children who were to work in pairs. The idea of menus can be adapted to projects and many other areas of the primary classroom.

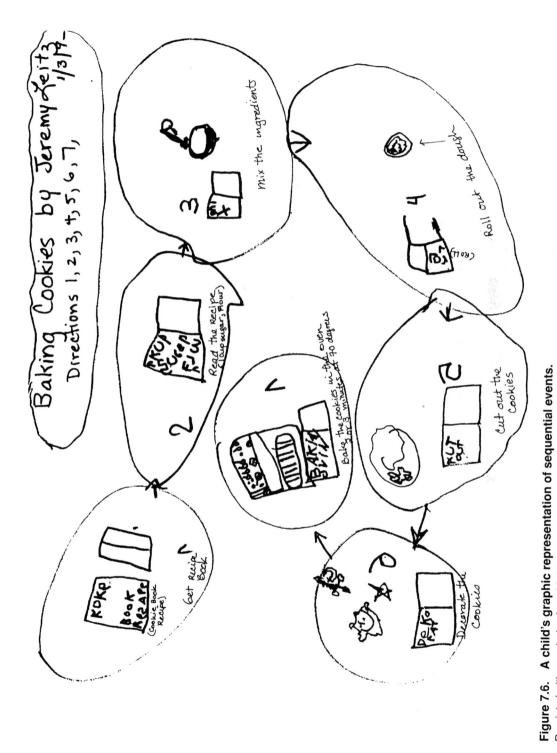

Figure 7.6. A child's graphic representation of sequential events.

Reprinted with permission from McAfee, O. and Leong, D. *Assessing and guiding young children's development and learning.* Copyright 1994 by Allyn and Bacon

Figure 7.7.   Child and teacher conferencing over a menu

Guidelines for Using External Mediators

Although Vygotsky first introduced the idea of external mediation in development and gave examples in informal settings, his students expanded and applied his ideas to the classroom. In particular, Zaporozhets (1959/1977), Venger (1969/1977, 1986), Elkonin (1971/1977), Gal'perin (1969), and their students and colleagues elaborated on the uses of external mediation. The following recommendations are distilled and adapted from their work.

To be effective, the external mediator must initiate the behavior at the right time. It must have the following characteristics.

1. *The mediator must have special meaning for the young child and be able to invoke that meaning.* The child must be able to touch or see the mediator, and it must elicit specific thoughts or behaviors. The child must be able to say, for example, "When I see the yellow sticker, I am supposed to remember to go to my recorder lesson today," "When I see the red hat, it means I have to wait and not interrupt the teacher," or "When the shades are drawn and the lights are low, it's time to rest." The mediator must have meaning to the child; it will not be useful if it has meaning only to the adult. The child may choose the mediator with adult help, but she may need coaching and practice in using it before it takes on the intended meaning. Once it has, the child should take some action to evoke the mediator. For example, the child must pick up the carpet square, put on the peace bracelet, or get the ticket. The act of mediation must be incorporated into the actions that occur as part of the activity.

2. *The mediator must be attached to an object that the child will use before or when performing the task.* If the goal is to remember to take home boots, the mediator must be attached to something the child looks at just before starting for home. It cannot be attached to something the child uses in the morning. If the child must remember something after lunch, then the mediator should be attached to the lunch box. If it is time to put toys away, use a special kind of music that is only played during cleanup time. If the alphabet line is to help children form letters as they write in their journals, the letters must be contained on a card the children have on their desks. The alphabet line on the bulletin board is too far removed from the child's activity to be a meaningful mediator for most children.

3. *The mediator must remain salient to the child.* Mediators will lose their distinctiveness and will no longer prompt appropriate behavior if they are used too much or for too long a time. The child cannot wear the stuffed animal that signals "Don't Grab" all day long; the mediator must be used under carefully controlled circumstances. Pick a specific time when the mediator will be most likely to stay salient. Do not have the child put it on first thing in the morning and wear it all day. Instead, have the child put on the mediator for a short period of time during which the child has trouble with a particular skill. For example, it is more effective for the child to wear the peace bracelet only during dramatic play or just before going out on the playground. Make the purpose of the mediator explicit, as in "We are going to put on this peace bracelet so it reminds you to use your words if you get angry!" Once the child succeeds in remembering successfully a number of times, the mediator should be removed.

4. *Combine mediation with language and other behavioral cues.* With the mediator use a set of behaviors that can become a habit and words that can become private speech to self-coach. For example, you might put up a picture of a light bulb right by the door of the classroom at the beginning of the morning to prompt focused attention. The light bulb is a symbol for a routine of pausing and saying in a whisper before entering "What am I supposed to remember to do today? I'm supposed to remember to listen and concentrate." Prompt the use of memory strategies by using a graphic picture of a child pointing to her temple. Bring the picture out when the children are supposed to remember something, such as bringing a book from home. Use the picture with words like "Let's put it in our memory bank by saying what we need to remember three times." Then both you and the children point at your temples and say "Bring a book from home to share." Soon the picture will prompt the strategy of repeating to oneself to remember.

5. *Choose a mediator that is within the child's ZPD.* For a mediator to work, it must be within the child's zone of proximal development and used by the child to direct his actions. Timothy's mother says "Don't do that!" when he approaches the light socket and begins to put his finger inside. The mother's words inhibit Timothy's behavior, but they are not what Vygotsky would call a mediator because Timothy does not use them to control his behavior himself. He merely obeys his mother. Since he obeys, we are able to conclude that the idea of "don't" is within his zone of proximal development, but it is not a mediator

because the behavior is being controlled from outside. "Don't" becomes a mediator when Timothy approaches the light socket, says "Don't" aloud, and does not put his finger in the socket, even when his mother is not around.

6. *Always use the mediator to represent what you want the child to do.* Be sure to coach the children on what you want them to *do* rather than just what you want them to stop doing. It is easier to replace a behavior than to inhibit one. Teaching children to say "Use your words" is much more effective than just telling them "Stop fighting."

In our work with teachers we are often asked what makes a good external mediator. We have found that pretty much anything will work as long as it is salient and doesn't blend into the background. Colored pens and pencils, stick-on notes, and menus (lists of things to do) help to remind children about directions or make aspects of the reading or writing process more salient. Tangible, moveable objects such as rings, bracelets, clothespins, or stuffed animals on pins or bracelets work best for social behaviors and attention and memory activities where children move around the room. To help children with controlling physical behaviors, such as leaning on others during circle time, the mediator has to give the child a physical or kinesthetic boundary, such as a chair or a carpet square. We have even used the teacher's picture as an external mediator to help a child who had trouble keeping on task during his homework. When he put the teacher's picture on his desk, he was able to get his homework done much more quickly.

Mediators exist in shared activity first. This means that adults provide the mediators when the child begins to learn. Initially, adults may find that they have to provide many different mediators. Teachers should not assume that one mediator will work for all the children. Lani is very distractable during group meeting time and requires maximum mediation before he is able to attend through a story. He does best when he sits on a carpet square with his name on it, with a stuffed animal on his lap, between two children who hold his hands during the story, and in front of the teacher (four mediators!). With this much mediation he is able to sit through the story. After successfully doing this for a week, the teacher begins to remove the mediators one by one. First Lani sits alone in front of the teacher on his carpet square with the stuffed animal. The next week he sits on his carpet square alone. Then 4 weeks later, the teacher takes his name tag off of the carpet square and Lani puts it on his arm; he no longer needs the physical reminder of the carpet square. Finally in five weeks he no longer needs the name tag either. The teacher carefully plans how she will take the scaffolding away.

The Value of Mediators

In the Vygotskian framework mediators make mental processing easier and more effective; they are the tools that enable children to eventually engage in higher mental processes. Mediators have both short-term and long-term value. In the short-term, mediators scaffold mental processing. Children having trouble focusing their attention are assisted if the teacher uses an external sign for attention. When the teacher puts on a set of rabbit ears to remind the children that they must pay close attention, the children listen better. If the teacher uses an egg timer with a loud tick and buzzer to signal cleanup time, children will stay focused on the task better. Otherwise children forget to clean and begin playing with the toys. The immediate effect of these external mediators is that the children accomplish a certain task more efficiently.

Mediators also have important long-term consequences because they are a means for both development and learning/teaching. Mediators provide the assistance necessary for the development of higher mental functions. By using mediators, children acquire deliberate memory, focused attention, and self-regulation. The use of mediators is a part of the definition of higher mental functions. Secondly, mediators are the means by which learning/teaching takes place. As the child moves through the ZPD, what the child can do with assistance becomes what the child can do independently. How does this movement occur? As the child internalizes mediators, he is able to improve his performance, and what originally belonged to the adult is appropriated by the child. In acquiring the mediator the child learns an entire set of behaviors. We can illustrate these principles by examining some classroom examples.

Scaffolded Writing Technique

Aaron can dictate a long story, but when he is asked to write on his own, he usually only writes a couple of letters. Sometimes the letters correspond with words he wants to write; sometimes they do not. Lately, he refuses to write anything down at all, preferring to spend his time adding to his drawings. Figure 7.8 shows an example of Aaron's independent writing.

The reason that Aaron is having trouble writing is that he lacks the focused attention and deliberate memory that are necessary for him to complete the task. When the appropriate mediators are provided, Aaron will be able to perform at a much higher level.

Aaron's teacher, Ms. Richards, decides to use the scaffolded writing technique to mediate writing and to help Aaron remember what he wants to write. She asks Aaron to dictate a story, but instead of writing the dictation the teacher makes a highlighted line for each of the words Aaron says.

The first time they use the highlighter, Ms. Richards draws the lines and models how Aaron can write his own words on the lines. After watching the teacher model how to do it, Aaron dictates a new sentence and then writes on the lines. Ms. Richards explains as she makes the lines, "They help you to remember what you want to write." She highlights lines for one sentence at a time.

Figure 7.9 shows what Aaron and the teacher did together. As the lines are drawn, the teacher and Aaron say the words together, and before Aaron begins writing, the teacher asks him to repeat back what he will put on the lines.

With the highlighted lines as a mediator, Aaron is able to write at a much more sophisticated level than he can unassisted. In addition, he makes more attempts to

Teacher and child plan a story together using the highlighter.

sound out the words and to use conventional spelling. The scaffolded writing technique helps him to remember in a more deliberate way. Notice in Figure 7.10 that even the penmanship and the spacing between the words have improved.

After using the highlighter with the teacher to plan his stories for about 1 week, Aaron begins to self-scaffold by using the highlighter by himself to plan his writing. He is observed talking to himself, and as he says each word he makes a line. After drawing the lines for himself and adding the punctuation, he fills in his words. Thus, the mediator of highlighting words with lines becomes a tool that he can use independently to increase his deliberate memory. Figure 7.11 shows Aaron's story planned and written on his own.

Scaffolded Reading

Melinda has been trying to learn short vowel sounds for the last three months. She still cannot reliably read these vowels without the teacher's prompting at each word. Even after having the sentence read to her, she cannot read it back with the correct vowel sounds. Three other children in the class have this same problem.

Melinda is having trouble focusing attention on the correct attribute as well as deliberately remembering this attribute throughout the whole task. When the teacher works one on one with her, Melinda is able to identify the correct vowel sound. As soon as she is asked to read alone or in a small group, however, Melinda is no longer able to perform.

In this case the level of assisted performance is attainable, but the problem is how to transfer responsibility from the teacher to the child. This is where external mediation is especially effective and useful. Scaffolded reading can bridge the gap, facilitating the child's performance without direct adult intervention or interaction.

Mr. Grey gives Melinda and the other three children laminated books and a highlighter and asks her to highlight all of the short *i* sounds as the group reads the

Figure 7.8. Aaron's independent writing before using the highlighter technique

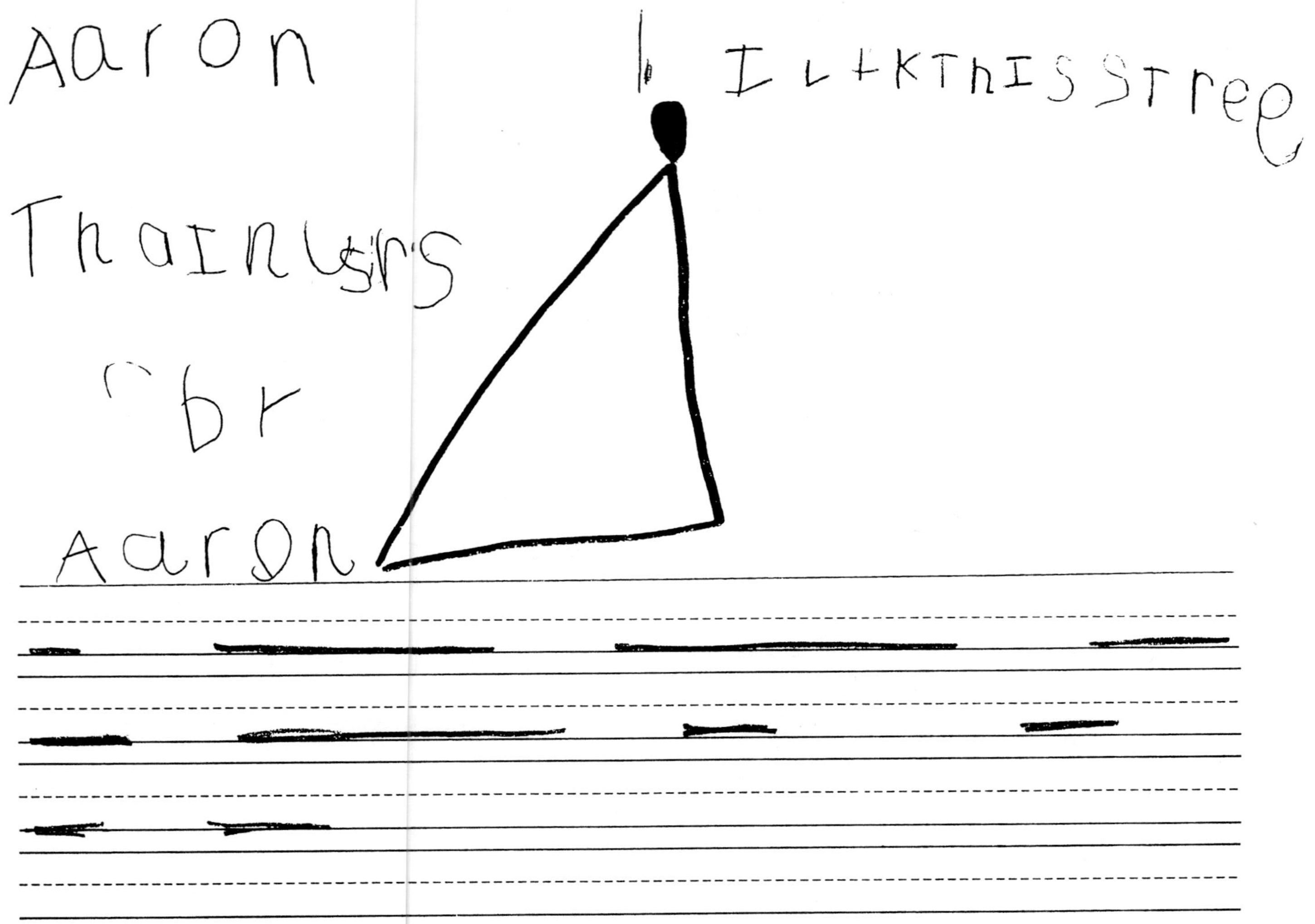

Figure 7.9. Lines drawn by teacher to highlight the words Aaron will write

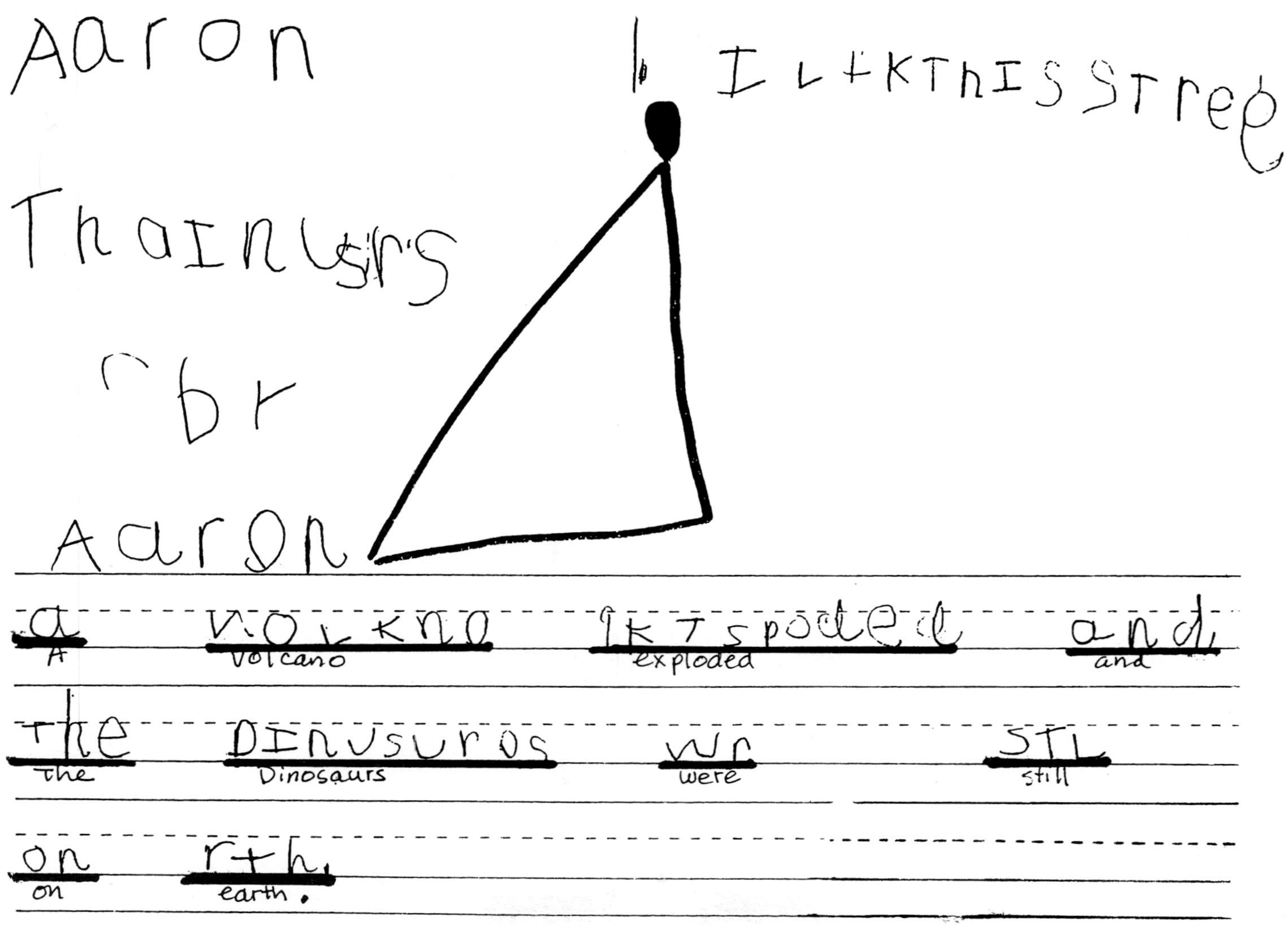

Aaron

I L+kthisstree

Thainusirs

rbr

Aaron

a vokno ikts posdet and
a   volcano explodeed   and   still
stl

the Dinvsvros wr
the   Dinosaurs   were

on rth.
on   earth.

Figure 7.10. Aaron's assisted writing after using scaffolded writing for 2 days

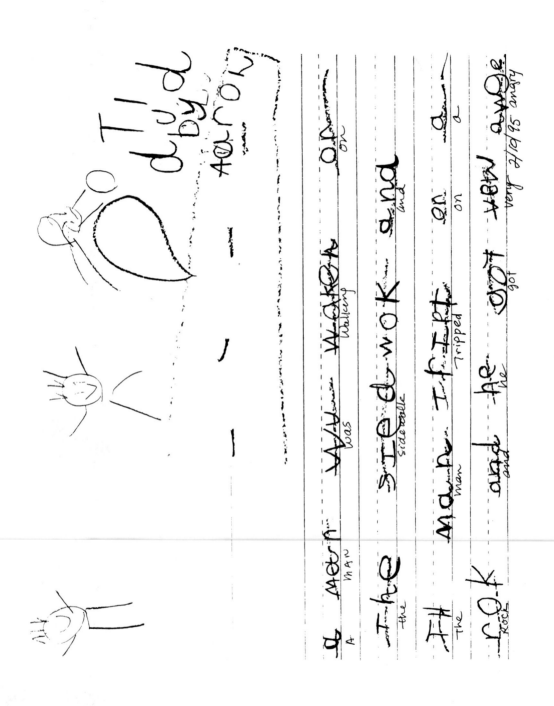

a morn a waken o
A   man   was walking on

The siedwok and
the   sidewalk   and

A mane trirpt on a
The   man   Tripped on

rok and he got mad
rock   and   he   got

very 2/10/95 angry

Figure 7.11. Aaron's self-scaffolded writing

Twinkle, twinkle, little star,
How I wonder what you are!
Up above the world so high,
Like a diamond in the sky.
Twinkle, twinkle, little star,
How I wonder what you are!

Figure 7.12. Using a highlighter to identify short *i* sounds during a group reading session

story. On the first page, the children and the teacher read each word and discuss whether or not it contains a short *i* sound before they mark it. On the second page, the group reads each vowel sound carefully and the children mark the word and discuss it after it is marked. By the third page, the children work in pairs reading for each other and marking as they read. By the end of the story, most of the children are able to reliably identify the short *i* sounds. Figure 7.12 shows one page where the highlighter was used.

The scaffolded reading technique enables Melinda to perform at an assisted level and also helps her to take responsibility for remembering by the last page. Thus she is able to appropriate the information more easily than by herself.

For Further Reading

Bodrova, E. & Leong, D. J. (1995). Scaffolding the writing process: The Vygotskian approach. *Colorado Reading Council Journal, 6,* 27-29.

Kozulin, A. (1990). *Vygotsky's psychology: A biography of ideas.* Cambridge: Harvard University Press.

Van der Veer, R., & Valsiner, J. (1991). *Understanding Vygotsky, A quest for synthesis.* Cambridge: Blackwell.

Venger, L. A. (1977). The emergence of perceptual actions. In M. Cole (Ed.), *Soviet developmental psychology: An anthology.* White Plains, NY: Sharpe. (Original work published in 1969)

Zaporozhets, A. V. (1977). Some of the psychological problems of sensory training in early childhood and the preschool period. In M. Cole & I. Maltzman (Eds.), *A handbook of contemporary Soviet psychology.* New York: Basic Books. (Original work published in 1959)

CHAPTER 8

Tactics: Using Language

Three-year-old Joe is baking pizza with the teacher but can't roll out the dough, so Mr. Sanchez says, "Roll the pin toward you and away from you." He is helping Joe feel the rolling pin moving back and forth. With this aid, Joe is immediately able to roll out the dough. As Mr. Sanchez moves away to help another child, he hears Joe sing "Toward . . . away . . . toward . . . away . . ." over and over again to himself as he rolls the pin over the dough.

Five-year-old Maura is counting objects. "There are eight of them," she says. The teacher adds one more to the pile and says, "I'm adding one, how many are there now?" Maura looks at the pile and then begins to count: "One, two, three, four, five, six, seven, eight, nine. There are nine now." The teacher adds another object, and Maura again starts counting from 1.

Six-year-old Jason is doing a movement exercise pattern of one jump and two hops. Jason says the pattern out loud, "Jump, hop, hop," as he does each step. He is so loud that the teacher asks him to stop talking because he is mixing everyone else up. The minute he stops, he cannot move. Only when all the other children finish and the teacher lets Jason resume his chant can he finish.

In all of these situations, children are using language to help them perform a behavior and to think. Language plays a central role in mental development. This is one of the four major principles of the Vygotskian paradigm. Language is a major cultural tool that enables us to think logically and to learn new behaviors. It influences more than just the content that we know; it also impacts thinking and the acquisition of new knowledge. In this chapter, we discuss how language develops and how teachers can use language to promote development and assist learning in the classroom.

Language as a Cultural Tool

Language is a universal cultural tool that is applied in many contexts to solve a myriad of problems. Vygotsky and many other theorists argue that language separates humans from animals, making humans more efficient and effective problem solvers. All humans in all cultures have developed language. Because humans possess language, they solve much more complex problems than primates who do not. In studies comparing problem-solving skills, researchers found that young toddlers and chimpanzees were similar in solving sensorimotor problems (e.g., Kozulin, 1990). However, once the toddlers acquired language, their problem-solving ability improved dramatically. Thereafter, the chimpanzees were not able to solve problems at the same level as the toddlers.

We use language in speaking, writing, drawing, and thinking. These manifestations of language are different, but they have some common features. Speech directed outward enables us to communicate with other people, and speech directed inward allows us to communicate to ourselves, to regulate our own behavior and thinking. We use writing to communicate with others, as well as a way to externalize and make our own thought processes tangible. Drawing and other graphic representations of our thinking serve a function similar to writing. Thinking is an inner dialogue in which we play out different perspectives, ideas, or concepts in the mind.

As a cultural tool, language is a distillation of the categories, concepts, and modes of thinking of a culture. Like some Western anthropologists and psycholinguists (Sapir, 1921; Wells, 1981; Whorf, 1956), Vygotskians believe that language shapes the mind to function in the most efficient way for a particular culture. Thus, Eskimo people have many words for snow, Guatemalan Indians who are weavers have many words for textures of yarn, and Asian cultures have many words to define familial relationships and kinships. Language reflects the importance of certain elements of the physical and social environment.

Language allows the acquisition of new information: content, skills, strategies, and processes. While not all learning involves language, complex ideas and processes can only be appropriated with the help of language. The idea of number is only internalized with the help of language. Through language, strategies for solving social conflicts are also taught.

Since language is a universal cultural tool, delays in its development have severe consequences. Language delays impact other areas of development: motor, social, and cognitive. Luria (1979) presents the case of two twins who had severe language delays because they had little interaction with others. These 5 year olds also had significant delays in social and problem-solving skills. Once their language abilities improved, the twins showed similar gains in the other areas of development. Research in special education also shows possible connections between language delays and problems in school.

The Functions of Speech

In the Vygotskian paradigm speech has two different functions (Zivin, 1979). *Public speech,* the term used for language directed at others, has a social, communicative function. It is spoken aloud and directs or communicates with others. Public speech can be formal, such as a lecture, or informal, such as a discussion over the dinner table. *Private speech* describes self-directed speech that is audible but not intended for others. This type of speech has a self-regulatory function.

Public speech and private speech emerge at different times. In infancy, speech primarily has a public function and is vital for adaptation to the social environment and learning. As the child grows, speech acquires a new function; it is not used solely for communication but also for helping the child to master his own behavior and acquire new knowledge. Not every concept the child learns proceeds through private speech, but many of them do. Young children establish relationships between concepts by trying different combinations of objects and ideas through private speech because they cannot silently consider these relationships.

Developmental Path of Speech

Vygotsky believed that the origins of speech are social, even from the very beginning in infancy. Both receptive and productive language have their roots in the social exchanges that occur between the child and the caregiver. Practically any infant vocalization is interpreted as social, as if the baby is communicating something. A parent engages in conversations with a baby even though the baby only responds with babbling and cooing sounds. Walk down a supermarket aisle behind a parent with a 6 month old and you might hear a discussion like this: "Should we buy rice or oatmeal?" "Ababaa." "Oh, sure, let's buy the oatmeal!" "abaaasajaa."

This interpreting of all vocalizations and gestures as social is a uniquely human trait. Even deaf parents treat infant gestures as conveying a message. Studies of chimpanzees taught American Sign Language found that the chimpanzee mothers never try to interpret the random behaviors and gestures of their babies as having communicative value (Kozulin, 1990).

Interpreting language as social is a view that is different from that of Piaget (1923/1926), who believed that speech reflects the child's present level of mental processing and is based on the child's schemas and internal representations. Using speech in social interactions follows these internal representations. In his early writings, Piaget (1923/1926) argued that speech begins by being extremely egocentric or even autistic, reflecting the general egocentrism of the preschool child's mind. Piaget's later views on the role of social interaction in the development of cognitive processes were modified to accommodate Vygotsky's ideas. Also, current theories of language development acknowledge the contributions of the social context (John-Steiner, Panofsky, & Smith, 1994).

The Emergence of Speech and Thinking

Vygotsky believed that there is a time in infancy and toddlerhood when thinking proceeds without language and language is used only for communication. Other psychologists, such as Piaget (1923/1926, 1952) and Bruner (1968), seem to concur that children go through a stage in which language is not essential to thinking or problem solving. Children solve problems with sensorimotor actions or by manipulating images rather than concepts or words. Language at this stage communicates wants and needs to others. For example, the word *Baba* may mean "I want my bottle." *Baba* is not used to stand for all bottles, as it may when the child is older. Vygotsky used the terms *preverbal thought* and *preintellectual speech* to describe this stage.

Then, between 2 to 3 years of age thinking and speech merge. From this point on, so Vygotsky believed, neither speech nor thinking would ever be the same. When thinking and speech merge, thinking acquires a verbal basis and speech becomes intellectual because it is used in thinking. Speech is then employed for purposes other than communication. After studying children using speech to solve problems, Vygotsky and Luria (1984/1994) drew this conclusion:

1. A child's speech is an inalienable and internally necessary part of the operation [of problem solving], its role being as important as that of action in the attaining of a goal. The experimenter's impression is that the child not only speaks about what he is doing, but that for him speech and action are in this case *one and the same complex psychological function* directed toward the solution of the given problem.
2. The more complex the action demanded by the situation and the less directed its solution, the greater the importance played by speech in the operation as a whole. Sometimes speech becomes of such vital importance that without it the child proves to be positively unable to accomplish the given task. (p. 109)

To put this into simpler language, children become capable of thinking as they talk. The child can think aloud. This idea is very different from talking after we think. Vygotsky believed that thinking and speaking occur simultaneously. He argues that in some cases, our external speech helps us form ideas that may exist only vaguely. Have you ever found yourself understanding your own thinking better when you talk it out with someone else? We may even say, "Can I talk to you about this so I can clarify what I think?"

When children become capable of thinking as they talk, speech actually becomes a tool for understanding, clarifying, and focusing what is in one's mind. After listening to a string of directions for the next activity, Juan turns to Sue and says, "She said to start with the red book." He confirms the teacher's directions and focuses his own attention. Thinking while talking makes shared activity doubly powerful. When children talk to each other as they work, their language supports learning, but the verbal interaction also helps each child to think while talking.

Private Speech

When speech and thinking merge, a special kind of speech emerges. This speech is what Vygotsky called private speech. Private speech is audible but directed to the self rather than to other people. It contains information as well as self-regulatory comments. It is the kind of thing that grown-ups do when faced with a difficult multistep task. We talk aloud to ourselves: "The first thing is to put the red rod into the red socket. Then the green rod fits into the spot marked with the green dot . . . ." Young children do this too, though more often than grown-ups. For example, Suzanne is playing at the computer and she says, "Need to move it here, then here—oops—then up. . ." as she maneuvers the mouse to move a small truck through an on-screen maze. Two-year-old Harold says to himself, "Orange-yellow, orange-yellow. . ." as he sorts blocks into groups.

Private speech is often abbreviated and condensed, unlike public speech, which communicates with others. Private speech sounds egocentric, as if the child doesn't care if she is understood by anyone else. Vygotsky points out that this egocentrism is not a deficiency of speech but an indicator of another function of speech at this age. It is not necessary for private speech to be completely explicit since it must only be intelligible to the child. The child has an intuitive sense of internal audience.

Piaget (1923/1926) calls such speech egocentric speech, and mostly focuses on its occurrence during *collective monologues* when several children are playing together. To Piaget, egocentric speech reflects the preoperational level of thinking, when the child has one worldview and cannot simultaneously take other perspectives. In collective monologues, each child holds a self-directed conversation at the same time, not caring whether the utterances are understood by others. With maturation, this type of speech disappears and is replaced by normal social speech when the child reaches the stage of concrete operations. For Piaget there is no relationship between egocentric speech and self-regulation (Zivin, 1979).

In a series of experiments, Vygotsky (1934/1987) showed that the collective monologue was not totally egocentric but social in nature. The rate of speech was greater in group situations than when children were alone. If speech were totally egocentric, the rate would remain the same regardless of how many children were near. Vygotsky argues that collective monologues and seemingly egocentric speech are an emerging form of private speech. This early private speech has external manifestations and is self-directed, but it may appear similar to communicative speech. For Vygotsky, private speech does not disappear with age, as Piaget suggested, but becomes less audible, gradually moving inside the mind, and becoming verbal thinking. In young children, the speech used for communication and for private speech is not easily distinguished and occurs simultaneously in the same context. Public and private speech gradually separate into two distinct strands in older children and adults.

Luria (1969), a colleague of Vygotsky, argues that private speech actually helps children make their behavior more deliberate. In a series of experiments, Luria found that general directions, such as "Squeeze two times," did not have an effect on the behavior of young children 3 to 3 $\frac{1}{2}$ years of age. Children would squeeze any number of times. However, when children were taught to say "Squeeze, squeeze" and this private speech was directly paired with action, the private speech helped the children to control their behavior.

Here is another example. Mr. Smith raises his hand and says, "When I lower my hand, you jump." All of the preschool children start jumping up and down even before he gets his hand ready. The result is different, however, when Mr. Smith says, "Let's say, all together, 'One, two, three, jump,' and we'll jump on 'jump.'" The class says the four words together, and they all jump only on the word "jump." Repeating the words rhythmically helps children to inhibit jumping at the wrong time.

A teacher might also use private speech to help a child with temper tantrums. Four-year-old Eric has a temper tantrum in the lunch line almost every day because he cannot wait his turn. As he walks to the lunchroom, his teacher rehearses what will happen. "You will *stand in line,* we will *count down* to your turn, you will *get a spoon, fork, food, and sit down.*" The teacher coaches Eric and prompts him to repeat what they will do, holding out one finger, then two, and then three for the three actions he must remember. When they get to the lunch line, the teacher and Eric both signal "one" with their index fingers, and the teacher listens to Eric say, "Stand in line." Then they give the signal "two" as Eric says, "Count down." They proceed to count together: "Two more people till Eric's turn. . . One more person till Eric's turn. . . Eric's turn." Then they signal "three" as Eric says, "Get my fork and spoon and food and sit." After a week, Eric needs few prompts except the finger signals, and there are no tantrums in the lunchroom. Three weeks later, the teacher no longer prompts him at all. Sometimes Eric holds onto his fingers to prompt himself and sometimes he does not.

Inner Speech and Verbal Thinking

Once speech separates into two distinct strands, private speech goes "underground" and becomes inner speech and then verbal thinking. The concepts of inner speech and verbal thinking describe different internal mental processes. *Inner speech* is totally internal, nonaudible, self-directed, and retains some of the characteristics of external speech. When people use inner speech to talk to themselves, they hear the words but do not say them aloud. For instance, when preparing for an important telephone call, you might mentally rehearse what you will say. Inner speech contains all of the things you might actually say, but it is an abbreviated version of the conversation. Inner speech in adults is similar to the private speech of preschoolers, because it is distilled, nongrammatical, and logical primarily to oneself.

Verbal thinking is more distilled than inner speech and is described by Vygotsky as *folded*. When thinking is folded, you can think of several things simultaneously and you may not be conscious of all that you are thinking. Although you may be aware of the final product, it takes a concerted mental effort to "unfold" or draw the ideas back into consciousness. Strategies, concepts, and ideas that exist in verbal thinking have been *automatized* (Gal'perin, 1969), they have been learned so well that they are automatic, not needing any conscious concentration to enact them. An adult immediately answers $2 + 2 = 4$. There is no thinking about the mental operation of addition. When a mother teaches her teenager to drive a car with a manual transmission, because shifting is so automatic to her, she has to sit in the driver's seat and go through the actions slowly to figure out the order in which the clutch and gas pedals are used.

Once something has been automatized, it can still be unfolded and reexamined. At times children and adults who have already developed verbal thinking may need to return to previous levels and engage in private and public speech (Tharp & Gallimore, 1988). When children are having trouble understanding something, it is particularly helpful to induce the reexamination of verbal thinking by having them explain things to others. Induced public speech helps the child think while talking, drawing out the folded ideas into a sequence. We have, ourselves, found that talking about Vygotsky often clarifies our understandings of complex concepts. By talking to each other we actually understand our own individual thoughts better.

In verbal thinking we may be unaware of flaws and gaps in our understanding. Have you ever read the definition of a word and thought you understood it, only to find out you cannot explain it in your own words to another person? Most of the time, an adult is able to sense a gap in understanding without having to discover it by talking aloud. Because children lack the higher mental functions, they are less likely to sense when they do not know or understand something. Without higher mental functions, they are not able to monitor their understanding unassisted. It is for this reason that teachers need to draw out children's thinking from its folded state. When teachers do this, they provide the assistance necessary for the child to reexamine his own thinking. Asking children to explain their thinking, think while talking to peers, and to write or draw their understandings are ways that teachers can assist the process of unfolding verbal thinking.

The Development of Meaning

Vygotsky also examined how children learn semantics, or the meaning of language. He believed that children construct meaning through shared activity. Meaning is a convergence between the adult's meaning and the child's inferences about what the adult means. Since meaning exists first in a shared state, contextual cues and the adult's strategies for interpreting the child support meaning. When the teacher asks a toddler to point to the bird on a page with a limited number of pictures, the context cues the child as to what a bird is. The child understands "bird" in that context but may not possess the same meaning for the word that the teacher does. For example, the child may point to a leaping frog as a bird on the next page.

As long as the child uses a word in familiar contexts while communicating with familiar adults, her understanding is sufficient to maintain conversation. Only when children try to apply meaning to different contexts and with different people does the difference between the child's meaning and the adult's become visible. Five-year-old Tamara uses the word *aunt* to describe all of her aunts correctly. However, she becomes confused when she meets a relative who is her niece and is actually older than she is. When her niece calls her "Auntie Tamara," she bursts into tears, saying, "I'm not an aunt, I'm a little girl."

Children and adults use the same words, but a child's meaning for a word will often be different from the adult's meaning. The younger the child, the more different the meaning. As the child interacts with different people, in different contexts, over different tasks, he restructures his initial personal meaning over and over again. Eventually, the meaning becomes similar to the culturally adopted or conventional meaning. Generally, the older the child, the more similar her meanings for everyday concepts will be to the adult's meanings. For example, 4-year-old Juan says, "Day is when I play, and night is for sleeping." As he grows older, his conceptions of day and night will become less personal and eventually will be similar to the conventional definitions of day and night.

Even when everyday concepts are learned later in life, the developmental path is the same. Meanings are constructed in context and then through many experiences are gradually restructured until they are similar to conventional cultural meanings. An everyday concept involves adding to and refining its meaning through daily experience. We do not place everyday concepts in an abstract system or define them formally. For adults this process moves more quickly than it does for children, but in either case everyday concepts are understood intuitively.

Learning is different when it comes to scientific concepts. Scientific concepts are not presented one at a time but as a whole system because the meanings are interdependent and cannot be acquired in isolation. For example, every science has its own basic assumptions and language. These are introduced as definitions that must be learned in order to understand the concepts of that science. The concepts only make sense when the child knows the basic assumptions and definitions. Thus, understanding the scientific concept of night and day requires knowing about the rotation of the earth. We usually teach science concepts in this integrated fashion when children are in junior high and high school, although several Russian researchers advocate the introduction of some scientific concepts in early primary grades and even in kindergarten (Davydov, 1991; Rubtsov, 1991).

Scientific concepts, Vygotsky says, "grow down" into existing everyday concepts, and everyday concepts "grow up" into scientific concepts (Karpov & Bradsford, 1995). Once children learn scientific concepts, their everyday concepts are restructured. If a child lacks background knowledge or if his everyday concepts do not match conventional meanings, then the child has trouble acquiring scientific concepts. For example, a child who does not have the everyday concepts of "more" and "less" could not understand the idea of "greater than" ($>$) and "less than" ($<$) when applied to numbers. Furthermore, learning scientific concepts causes children to become more systematic in their use of everyday concepts. Once a child has learned that there is a difference between stars, planets, and moons, stargazing takes on a different meaning.

An example of the difference between everyday and scientific concepts is shown in Mr. Johnston's second-grade class. In class he asks children to generate a list about what they know about the rain forest. This list is a catalogue of the children's everyday concepts about the rain forest. The children write things like "It has trees," "We cut the logs and then ruin the land," "The birds die because they don't have a place to live," and "I like the rain forest." Mr. Johnston then presents information about the rain forest in the form of related scientific concepts. He discusses the rain forest as an ecosystem with specific characteristics that make it different from other ecosystems, and he explains the effects of destruction of habitat on the survival of animal and plant species. After studying the rain forest in a project, the children are asked to write down what they now know. Mr. Johnston can see that the scientific concepts are growing into the everyday ones because children are beginning to use scientific language in their writing. Now they write things like "It is a habitat with dense trees and lots of raining," "It is not a desert," and "There are many kinds of plants and animals living there." The scientific concepts have altered the way the children think about the idea of rain forest. At the same time, the children's intuitive concepts were used to build the scientific ones.

The Development of Written Speech

Vygotsky reserved a special place for written speech in the development of higher mental functions. Written speech is not just oral speech on paper but represents a higher level of thinking. It has a profound influence on development because

1. it makes thinking more explicit
2. it makes thinking and the use of symbols more deliberate
3. it makes the child aware of the elements of language

How Writing Promotes Thinking

Written speech makes thinking more explicit. Like spoken speech, written speech forces inner thoughts into a sequence because you can say or write only one idea at a time. Forced to be sequential, you can no longer think about several things simultaneously. Written speech also forces you to unfold inner speech, but unlike the spoken word, writing allows you to literally look at your thoughts. When we speak, our thoughts exist for the moment we say them. When we write, our thoughts are recorded and can be revisited and reflected upon. Gaps in understanding become more apparent when you reread your thoughts. Another characteristic of written speech is that it is more elaborated and thus more context-free than spoken speech. Written speech must contain more information because there are no contextual cues to rely on when interpreting it. You cannot assume any common knowledge with your reader, and gesture and tone of voice cannot help you convey your meaning. As a child learns to write, he learns to take on the role of the reader, to see his thoughts as if for the first time. This gives the child even greater ability to see any gaps in his thinking and to notice any points of confusion in communicating those thoughts to others. After writing, our ideas are more explicit and elaborate than they were before. We see the flaws in our ideas more clearly and more objectively. Thus, for Vygotskians, writing improves thinking in a way that talking cannot.

Advocates of his perspective encourage the use of writing to help children structure and clarify new ideas. They make writing an integral part of the learning of all new content and skills. Children are encouraged to write about their understanding of a math problem as well as to solve the problem. Children write about their observations of a caterpillar in addition to making drawings and talking about what they see. By revisiting our thoughts on paper with others and by ourselves, we come to a deeper understanding of those thoughts.

Written speech also makes thinking and the use of symbols more deliberate. Because the child chooses the symbols she uses and must record them according to the laws of syntax, writing is a more deliberate process than talking. In the Vygotskian view, the choice of the symbols we use when we talk can be unconscious and with minimal consideration of the effect on the listener (the proverbial foot in the mouth!). The decontextualized nature of writing means that symbols must be chosen carefully. In oral speech, tone of voice, gesture, and common context can fill in the gaps. When someone doesn't understand something, we keep adding information until they get it. In written speech, only what is on paper communicates, so one's words must be chosen more deliberately. Thus, you are much more likely to play with different ways of saying the same thing when communicating on paper than when you are talking to someone.

Finally, written speech makes the child aware of the elements of the language. There are uniform rules governing relationships between sounds and symbols, between different kinds of words, and between ideas in a paragraph. While children may form some rudimentary ideas about the structure of language as they acquire metalinguistic awareness, these ideas become crystallized as the child learns to read and write. Meili has a vague understanding that words make up sentences, but when she sees sentences on a page, the idea of "word" becomes even clearer.

Drawing and Scribbling in Young Children

Young children who have not yet learned how to write, Vygotskians believe, represent their thoughts in the form of drawings and scribblings. These early representational skills are no less a tool to promote thinking than actual writing (Luria, 1979). This idea was tested in two early childhood programs, in Russia and in Italy. Vygotskian scholar Leonid Venger created an experimental curriculum for Moscow preschools that emphasized the development of representational skills. Another early childhood educator, Loris Malaguzzi, came up with his own interpretation of Vygotskian ideas that were successfully applied in preschools in Reggio Emilia in northern Italy (Edwards, Gandini, & Foreman, 1993).

Like Piaget (1923/1926), Venger (1986) argues that drawing is a representation of the child's thinking. Unlike Piaget, Venger asserts that the lack of specificity in the child's representation occurs because the child produces a model of the object which includes only its essential parts. As the child learns more about the object, his drawings of it will change, reflecting his newfound understanding. Piaget believed that the lack of specificity is due to the child's cognitive immaturity; as the child grows older, the drawings will become more detailed.

According to Venger, drawings can be used in the same way as writing. Drawing can increase a child's awareness of her own thinking. Having the child add details or redraw models will help the child think while drawing, thus increasing the child's understanding (Brofman, 1991). A similar technique has been used by teachers at Reggio Emilia to deepen children's understandings of space, time, and measurement (Edwards, Gandini, & Foreman, 1993). American educators who have visited this program have been impressed not only with the quality of the children's drawings but also the children's understanding of the subject matter.

Venger also suggests that drawing teaches children other cultural tools, such as how to express perspective and two-dimensional space. There are cultural conventions for how to draw objects that are near or far away and objects that are three-dimensional. This varies by culture. For example, in Western art, objects that are far away are drawn smaller than the ones that are nearer in space to the viewer. In Mongolian art, objects near and far are drawn the same size, but those far away are placed higher up on the page. By drawing and looking at drawings in books, children acquire these conventions and begin to apply them to their own work by 8 years of age.

As with drawing, scribbling and early attempts at writing have benefits that are similar to full-blown writing. Luria (1979) found that preschool children as young as 3 years of age begin to use prewritten speech in the same ways that adults use written speech. Three-year-olds used their scribbles to help them remember something or to label an object. These scribbles contained no real letters, nor were they understood by anyone but the child. Luria found that the children, nevertheless, gave these scribbles meaning and could remember the meaning several days later. Children thus begin to master the purpose of written speech long before they actually learn to write. Luria's ideas in this area had an influence on the development of the whole language movement for teaching reading (e.g., Teale & Sulzby, 1986; Schickedanz, 1982) as well as other methods of teaching reading through writing (e.g., Clay, 1991).

Using Language in the Classroom

From the Vygotskian approach, we can identify several ways to enhance children's use of language when teaching in the classroom.

1. *Make your actions and the children's actions verbally explicit.* Label your own actions as you carry them out. Label the child's actions for him as they occur. The more you tie language to action, the more you will help children use language to facilitate learning. Avoid vague relational terms such as "these things" or "those." Use explicit terms, as in "Hand me the blue blocks" or "See the small furry squirrel puppet?" Teachers must also help children label their own behavior. Don't be afraid to say "You're not paying attention" or "I can see your mind is wandering." If children don't seem to know what you mean by "paying attention," you will have to describe it more fully or even practice it. You might say, "When you pay attention, your mind is like a beam of light and it shines only here" or "When you pay attention your body is still and does not wiggle, your eyes are here, and you are thinking about this book."

2. *Model your thinking and the strategies you are using aloud.* As you solve a problem, talk about what you are thinking about. Ms. Kaplan asks, "Which of these objects is bigger?" The children look puzzled. None of them responds. Ms. Kaplan then says, "Gee, I wonder how I might figure this out. Oh, I could put them together." She puts the objects next to each other and says, "If I look across, I can see that this one is bigger. What do you see?" Talking about strategies and giving several options will help children appropriate "hidden" thinking strategies.

3. *When introducing a new concept, be sure to tie it to actions.* It helps the child when you introduce a concept in context and demonstrate the action of the object or your action upon the object. Include as many cues as you can. For example, when introducing a ruler, Ms. Brady says, "When we want to measure something to see how long it is, we put the ruler at the end of the object and read the numbers here." As she speaks, she models how to do this by placing the ruler at the very edge of the object.

4. *Use thinking while talking to check children's understanding of concepts and strategies.* Get children used to talking about what they think and how they solve problems. Have them repeat ideas back to you or show you how they understand an idea. As one teacher puts it, "I need to know how you think about things." Have children talk to each other; then listen to what they say to each other. Not only is your listening motivating for children, it gives you wonderful insights into what they understand.

5. *Use different contexts and different tasks as you check whether or not children understand a concept or strategy.* When you teach a concept or strategy, it is always embedded in a specific social context. It is difficult to know whether or not a child understands the concept because there are so many contextual clues that the child can reuse. To assess whether or not a child understands something, you must change contexts so that a new facet of the concept is exposed.

You can do this by having the child interact with a peer (real or imaginary) or by changing tasks (counting cookies instead of bears).

6. *Encourage the use of private speech.* Encourage children to use private speech to help them learn. Children can whisper to themselves or sit in a place where private speech will not bother others. Private speech may sometimes seem to be unrelated to the task at hand. However, if the child is able to perform the task with the speech, she should be allowed to continue. For example, Josie is sitting at her desk talking and humming to herself but is able to stay on task. This type of self-talk has meaning for the child and should not be discouraged. If the humming doesn't assist with task completion, then you might try prompting appropriate private speech. Private speech is abbreviated, so children may translate directions into a one- or two-word prompt for themselves.

7. *Use mediators to facilitate private speech.* For some children, having an external mediator encourages private speech. Coach the child on what he might say to himself as he does something. If the child abbreviates this but is able to do the task, then let him continue to use the speech. For Alexei, having a card on his table with the numbers 1, 2, and 3 written on it helps him to remember which learning center he is to go to first, second, and third. The note prompts him to say to himself, "First I go to reading, then the listening center, then to the water table." One teacher uses the idea of having a place in your head called a memory bank. When children need to remember something, she says " We have to put this in our memory bank (pointing to her forehead). Let's say it three times and put it in. Ready? 'Bring a book to school tomorrow' (pointing to her forehead). 'Bring a book to school tomorrow' (pointing to her forehead). 'Bring a book to school tomorrow'" (pointing to her forehead). A very high percentage of her children remember the book.

8. *Encourage "thinking while talking".* Some children need to talk things through as they complete a task, even before they do it alone. This strategy provides the assistance some children need to help them look at their own thinking. Seven-year-old Jolinda cannot identify grammar mistakes in her daily language-conversations activity. No matter how many times she reads it to herself, "he wented" sounds just fine. Only when she reads it aloud to her grammar buddy does she discover the mistake.

9. *Encourage children to write to communicate even if it is scribbling.* Encourage children to write even if they do not use real letters. You can invite a child to draw or scribble and then write down in notes for yourself what the child says her writing means, or you can write the meaning underneath the child's representations as she dictates. Stickers can be used to stand for ideas, too. A sticker of a book, or a drawing of a book, for example, can be used to remind children to read.

10. *Encourage the use of written speech in a variety of contexts.* Don't confine writing to journals or a writer's workshop. In the elementary school classroom, use writing for math, science, reading, and art. Have children write about what

they have learned, even if it is just a word or a letter. These reflections will help you understand what the child knows and will help the child look at his own thinking.

11. *Revisit the children's writing and reprocess their ideas.* Revisit the child's writings, even if they are pictures with scribbles and dictated information. Talk about what the child might add to his writing or drawing after further thinking or studying. Use peers to reprocess the ideas represented. Have the child share the writing with a peer, such as during an "author's chair" activity. Coach the peers on what to say and questions to ask about the story. Write the responses down and use these to rediscuss the story. Ask children to redraw a picture of an object after they have examined it with a magnifying glass.

12. *Incorporate writing into play.* Place the tools for writing in the dramatic play area and suggest ways that children might use writing in their play. Children can write out the orders for their play restaurant, write in a journal as they play school, or draw out the plans for a city as they play with blocks. Acting out stories with peers will also encourage the use of language and writing.

For Further Reading

Berk, L. E., & Winsler, A. (1995). Scaffolding children's learning: Vygotsky and early childhood education. NAEYC Research and Practice Series, 7. Washington DC: National Association for the Education of Young Children.

Luria, A. R. (1976). *Cognitive development: Its cultural and social foundations* (M. Lopez-Morillas & L. Solotaroff, Trans.). Cambridge, MA: Harvard University Press.

Luria, A. R. (1979). *The making of mind: A personal account of Soviet psychology,* (M. Cole & S. Cole, Trans.). Cambridge, MA: Harvard University Press.

Vygotsky, L. S. (1962). *Thought and language* (E. Hanfmann and G. Vakar, Trans.). Cambridge, MA: MIT Press. (Original work published in 1934)

Vygotsky, L. S., & Luria, A. (1994). Tool and symbol in child development. In R. van der Veer & J. Valsiner (Eds.), *The Vygotsky Reader* (T. Prout and R. van der Veer, Trans.). Oxford: Blackwell. (Original work published in 1984)

CHAPTER 9

Tactics: Using Shared Activities

Zoe and Arlene are playing at the water table filling up different-size jugs with water. As they play, the teacher says, "I wonder how many smaller jugs of water it will take to fill up this large jug?" Zoe says, "I think three." Arlene shouts, "No, only one!" The teacher says, "Let's see. Let's use these blocks (small cubes) to stand for each bottle we measure. Zoe, you pour into the small jug, and Arlene, you put a block in this basket to stand for one small bottle. You'll do it each time, OK?" The teacher watches as the children empty water from the large, filled jug into the small jugs and put the blocks in the basket. The children count aloud as Arlene moves the block over. Once they pour until water spills out of a smaller jug, and the teacher says, "You have to fill it exactly and not spill or else we won't be measuring correctly." They re-fill the big jug and start over again. They gradually empty the large jug.

"There are three," Arlene says. "See." She points to the four blocks. The teacher pulls the basket closer and says, "Let's count these to make sure there are three." Arlene picks up a block and puts it in the teacher's open hand each time. "Oh, there are four" she says. "Yes," the teacher says, "sometimes it helps to point to the blocks or to pick them up when you count." Arlene says to Zoe, "Now I want to pour and you measure." After another cycle, Zoe looks at the basket of blocks, picks each one up as she counts and hands them to Arlene. "There are still four," Zoe says to Arlene and the teacher. "Yes," the teacher says, "it doesn't seem to matter who does the pouring, there are still four. Let's draw what we have learned about the difference between the big jug and the small jug." After they make the drawing, the teacher hangs it over the water table. The teacher encourages other children to "read" the drawing and "test out" what Zoe and Arlene have discovered.

It is within everyday exchanges such as this that learning occurs. We can easily recognize when such learning has occurred, but it is difficult to know what to do to make it happen. What can teachers do to increase the learning/teaching dialogue? This question is one that many American and Russian researchers have focused on. In this chapter, we will describe some of the recommendations derived from their applied research.

Interaction During Shared Activity

In Chapter 1 we explained Vygotsky's idea that mental functions can be shared; that is, they exist in shared activity. A mental function exists, or is distributed, between two people before it is appropriated and internalized.

There are a variety of ways in which an activity can be shared by two people. A child may use the strategy or concept with the support of another person. Two children may work together to solve a problem. One child may ask questions and another answer. In the earlier example of filling jugs with water, Zoe and Arlene share the strategy with the teacher as a trio.

The word *assistance* is an essential part of the definition of the zone of proximal development, or ZPD (see Chapter 4). Thus, shared activity is a means of providing the assistance children need at the higher levels of the ZPD. To promote learning, teachers must create different types of assistance and consequently different types of shared activity.

Because so many of examples of shared activity are adult-child exchanges, there are several misconceptions about what shared activity means. First, shared activities are not limited to adult-child interactions. Vygotsky's ideas about shared activity and its role in development go much beyond the adult-directed learning (Tharp & Gallimore, 1988). The social context includes many kinds of interactions between more and less knowledgeable participants, participants with equal knowledge, and even imaginary participants (Newman, Griffin, & Cole, 1989; Salomon, 1993). Each type of shared activity supports a different facet of development. In this chapter we will show how each type of shared activity can contribute to learning.

A second misconception is that the adult directs the child and the child is relatively passive. No learning occurs if the learner is not active. All participants, whether they are equal or unequal in knowledge, must be mentally engaged, or the activity will not be shared.

Finally, there must be a medium of sharing. Playing next to each other is not enough. The participants must communicate with each other by speaking, drawing, writing, or in some other way. Without rich verbal, written, or other kinds of exchanges, sharing will not produce the highest level of assistance possible. Language and interaction create the shared experience.

How Shared Activity Promotes Learning

Shared activity provides a meaningful social context for learning. When a child is first learning a skill, the social context may be the only thing that makes the learning meaningful. The child may try to learn simply because interacting with the teacher is very enjoyable. Social interaction provides support in a physical sense as well as a motivational sense. A beginning reader may resist reading two pages when it is assigned by the teacher, but the same child may be willing to read an entire book to a younger sister. Thus the shared activity of reading to someone else supports the emerging skills in a way that the reading assignment by itself cannot. The child's motivation is much stronger and the interaction provides actual practice and an appropriate social context for the acquisition of the skill.

Through talking and communicating, the gaps and flaws in one's thinking become explicit and accessible to correction. Once concepts are internalized, they may exist in a folded state and thus mistakes are not easily revealed. Children may be able to come up with an answer but have only a vague understanding of how they got it. In talking, writing, or drawing for someone else, thought becomes sequential and visible to the thinker. For example, after making butter in class, Steven can only vaguely describe what happened. However, as he plays house with Ty, he begins to pretend to make butter using actions in the same order that they occurred in class. The ensuing argument with Ty over whether to shake the jar first or look at the directions in the recipe helps both children to clarify the steps in the process.

In a preschool class that observed a building being constructed in the lot across from the school, the children try to explain to a new child what has happened. As they talk, the children clarify the sequence of events. When a child has solved a math problem and explains the answer to the teacher, she realizes that she made a mistake in the calculation.

Shared activity forces the participants to clarify and elaborate their thinking and to use language. To communicate with another person you have to be clear and explicit. You have to turn your idea into words and talk until you believe the other person understands you. You are forced to look at different aspects of an idea or task and to take another person's perspective. As a result, more and more sides or characteristics of an object or idea are exposed.

Shared Activity, Other-Regulation, and Self-Regulation

One of the things that happens in shared activity is that individuals take turns regulating and being regulated by others. This regulating and being regulated occurs at different levels in different types of shared activity. For example, in a sorting task where the teacher is more responsible for the interactions, the child will mainly be regulated by the teacher and the teacher will be regulated to a lesser degree by the child. The teacher tells the child what to do, but the child also regulates the teacher's actions by his responses. For example, a teacher may tell a child to put the large circles in one pile and the small circles in another pile. To engage in shared activity, the child will do as the teacher asks. When the child places the blue circles together, ignoring their size, this information regulates the teacher's reaction. Instead of moving on to the next task, he might say, "Ignore the color; just look at the size," or he might provide mediation to highlight the size.

In shared activities with peers or those in which the child is performing at an independent level, being regulated by others and regulating others will occur more evenly. In preparing a dramatic play, for example, children will discuss and argue about what roles they will play and how the play situation will develop. Sometimes a child will agree to a role or scenario that was suggested by another child; then the same child may insist on the role or scenario that she has suggested.

The Importance of Other-Regulation

Learning to be both the regulator and the object of regulation is important for the development of higher mental functions. Vygotskians believe that other-regulation precedes self-regulation (Leont'ev, 1978; Vygotsky, 1983). Children learn to regulate the behavior of other people before they are capable of regulating themselves. Many examples of this can be seen in preschool classrooms. Children around 3 or 4 years of age seem to be obsessed with rules and spend a great deal of their time telling the teacher when other people are not following the rules. This tattletaling is a symptom of the desire to regulate others. The tattleteller usually does not apply the rule to himself, but will be the first one to shout when someone else does wrong. The child wants to reaffirm the rule. For young children, the rule and the person who enforces it are the same: "I take just one cookie because the teacher said so." "I am quiet because the teacher said to be quiet." What children learn by using the rule to regulate others is the idea that the rule is abstract and exists apart from the person who enforces it. Once there is a rule, then it can be applied in other situations and the child begins to internalize that rule or to develop a standard. Instead of having to be reminded each time there are cookies that you take only one, the child now has a rule: "When there are cookies or any food, you take only one at a time." Likewise, the internalized rule about being quiet might be "I need to use a quieter voice when I am inside."

Using Other-Regulation to Promote Self-Regulation

Many of the things that children learn are rule-based, not only social interaction, classroom behavior, and play. Addition, spelling, reading—almost everything taught in school—involves using rules. In school we learn rules and standards as well as concepts and strategies.

Because children learn other-regulation first, they often can see the rule more easily when looking at the mistakes of another person, such as a classmate, than when trying to perform themselves. When they are doing something themselves, they may lose sight of the rule, but the rule jumps out at them when they see someone else's work. Have you have ever noticed how easy it is to edit another person's work? The typos and flaws in thinking are obvious. When you read your own writing, problems and mistakes are much harder to catch.

Teachers can use other-regulation to encourage the development of self-regulation by placing children in the position of regulating others. Some specific recommendations are given below.

1. *Plan exercises in which children have to identify mistakes in the teacher's work or in written exercises.* Presenting written sentences that have one or two grammatical or punctuation mistakes in them is useful in first and second grade. Be sure that you tell the children how many mistakes are in the sentence. Teachers can also make mistakes on purpose as they write sentences on the board for the children to correct. Children may not see the mistake at first because they think that teachers don't make mistakes. You will have to prompt them to see it at first.

2. *Plan activities in which the target child regulates other people using the target behavior.* Give the target child the responsibility for regulating the behavior you want him to learn. In Mr. Timothy's classroom, Jason's loud voice can be heard over all of the children, and it seems to increase the noise level to the point that some children hold their ears! Attempts to correct him by saying "Lower your voice" seem to have absolutely no effect on Jason. Mr. Timothy has even tried using a video recording to show Jason how much louder his voice is than those of the other children. None of his attempts has worked. Then Mr. Timothy puts a "noise meter" on the board (see Figure 9.1) and encourages Jason to identify when any person's noise level is too loud. Jason picks on everyone, including Mr. Timothy, mercilessly, pointing out when anyone speaks in a slightly raised voice. After 3 days, Mr. Timothy notices that when he asks Jason to lower his voice that he actually responds by lowering his voice! Vygotskians would argue that Jason

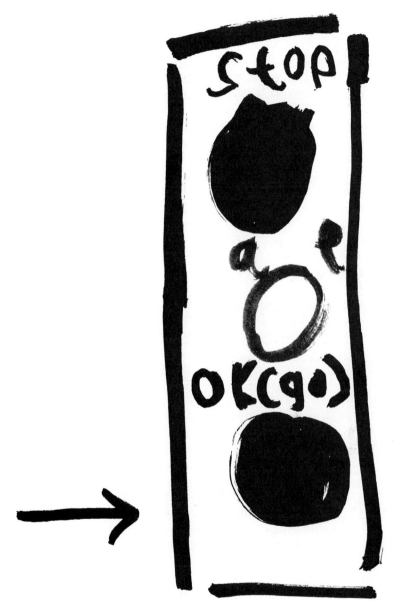

Figure 9.1.   Jason's noise meter

has begun to internalize a standard for what a lower voice is. Before, he responded to Mr. Timothy as if his request were just a whim. After regulating everyone else, Jason began to see that lowering your voice meant something specific.

3. *Pair other-regulation and self-regulation with an external mediator.* Use external mediators to trigger the behavior you want the children to use to regulate others

or themselves. In the above example, the teacher used a noise meter to help the children remember what they are supposed to do with their voices.

The Role of the Teacher in Shared Activity

A teacher may take part in a shared activity in two different ways: as a direct participant and as the person who promotes, plans, and creates the opportunities for shared activity to develop with others. In classroom activities teachers may assume both of these roles depending on the goals, contexts, and content of what is being taught. Sometimes only adults can guide and direct learning, but there are times when working with peers is more beneficial. Whether the teacher should directly participate in the activity depends on a number of factors such as where in the learning cycle the children are, the characteristics of specific children, the children's ages, and the group and its dynamics. For example, a peer discussion among a group of 5-year-olds might lead them to want to know more and to ask questions that can be answered on their own as well as questions that can be answered only by the teacher (Palincsar, Brown, & Campione, 1993). In this situation, the teacher plays the role of both planner and participant. At other times, direct teacher questions can prompt the same interest and learning, so direct participation produces the best motivation. Astute teachers know that they must use a variety of techniques and constantly change the form of presentation and amount of guidance as learning emerges in different children.

Teachers as Partners

One way that teachers participate in shared activity is by engaging in what Vygotskians call *educational dialogue* (Newman, Griffin, & Cole, 1989). The word *dialogue* implies give and take between all participants. Thus, a lecture, given to students is not an example of an educational dialogue. In an educational dialogue the children express their own understandings of what the teacher says and of the concept presented. This dialogue can involve written and drawn representations as well as speech.

An educational dialogue is similar to a *Socratic dialogue,* in which the teacher has a goal in mind and uses questions to guide the students toward that goal. It is not a free-flowing discussion but a teacher-guided journey of discovery. It is the children who must discover the meaning, but the teacher gently leads them to it, helping them correct misconceptions and avoid dead-end lines of thinking.

To engage in an educational dialogue, the teacher must have a concept or goal in mind and must be able to anticipate the possible misunderstandings that will emerge. She must guide, but the child must act and construct her own understanding. An analogy would be driving to a new destination. You drive at your own speed and make your own decisions about where to turn, but the road signs along the way provide useful information and anticipate your possible wrong turns. Along the road of learning, the teacher is the one who places the signs at the most useful and important points and makes sure you do not miss an important turn.

By asking questions, the teacher models the logic of learning, or the strategies that children can use to reach a solution next time. Put another way, the teacher constructs a template for learning that can be used in other situations. Ms. Osborne is looking at a new science book with her children. Winona asks, "Does it talk about bears?" Ms. Osborne says, "Let's see. Where can we look?" Sam says, "Let's look at the pictures." Ms. Osborne says, "We could look at pictures—that would tell us if it has bears in it—but I know a quicker way. We can look for the word *bears* in the index at the back of the book." Pointing to the columns she says, "The index tells you all of the topics covered. See how it's alphabetized. Where could we find bears?" "Under *B*," several children say. "Right. Where is the *B* section?" she asks as she turns the book so that one child can turn the page. "Yes, I see *B*'s now," she says as the child successfully finds the *B* section. Ms. Osborne turns the book toward another child and says, "Can you find *bears?*" The child points to the correct line. "Follow along with your finger and you'll see a page number. . . . Bears are discussed on page 78." If Ms. Osborne had simply said "yes" or turned to the page without leading the children through the process, they would not have been exposed to a strategy for finding information in a book.

In contrast to Piaget, Vygotsky believed that logic is learned through interaction with others. Piaget believed that logic is transparent and contained in the objects and operations performed on the objects (Beilin, 1994). He also maintained that culturally transmitted knowledge affects only the content of knowledge, not the operations used in thinking. Vygotsky believed that logical relationships are culturally based and transmitted through shared activities. Only when the teacher makes these relationships explicit, through questions or descriptions, does the child appropriate logic. Exploring and manipulating objects are not sufficient for the emergence of logical thought; children have to be taught these relationships.

Although the teacher has a goal in mind, the actual questions and steps used in the educational dialogue must be chosen anew with each child or group of children. Each child comes to the dialogue with a unique background and understandings, so the questions that lead to understanding for one child may not work with another. The teacher must keep in mind that children must participate in the dialogue for it to teach them anything because they must construct their own meaning (see Chapter 1).

One purpose of the educational dialogue is for the teacher to discover what the child understands and what assistance will work best. Because the learner does not really understand the final goal until she has mastered the skill or concept, it is difficult for the learner to articulate what part of the final concept she understands. This is something that only the teacher, who knows the final goal, can tell the child.

The teacher must answer two questions about the child's thought process: (a) how did the child arrive at this answer? and (b) will the child's answer ultimately fit into the system of concepts for this area? For Vygotskians, it is not enough just to reach the right answer; the child must use the tools that are most relevant to finding the answer. For example, it is more important for the child to be able to describe the pattern in a series of objects than to predict the next object. Knowing only which object comes next does not tell the teacher whether or how the child understands the pattern.

The second thing the teacher must discover in the educational dialogue is whether the child's answer will ultimately fit into the system of concepts for a specific area. The teacher has to keep in mind the entire system of learning. She must make sure that each new concept builds toward understanding of the entire system and does not create problems later. Ms. Berk goes over the elements of the calendar every school day. When she asks the children how many days there are in a week, she discovers that some of the children think there are 5 days. She asks the children to show her how there are 5 days. The children name the 5 days she usually discusses. Through her dialogue with the children, she discovers that they define the days of the week by the days they are in school. She then goes over the idea that there are 7 days in a week because she knows that their current misconception will lead to problems later.

As teachers participate in the educational dialogue, they need to keep these points in mind.

1. *Help the child distinguish between essential and nonessential properties.* For example, when showing children objects of different shapes, the teacher should demonstrate that color and size are irrelevant. She would ask the child, "If we paint this object red, is it still a circle?" "If we paint the circle blue, is it now a triangle?" "What if we make it bigger? Is it still a circle?"

2. *Help the child make connections with the larger system of concepts.* Susan points to the number 2 and says, "It's the letter two." The teacher engages her in a dialogue by asking, "Is this a letter or a number?" Susan says, "It's a letter like this" (pointing to an *A*). The teacher then says, "We write both letters and numbers, but we use them differently. How many fingers do I have up?" Susan says, "Two." The teacher says, "Yes, we would write that with a number because we use numbers to tell 'how many.' We use letters to make words."

3. *Look for clues about the child's thinking process.* Using the child's responses, try to identify the properties that are salient. The teacher asks the children, "What rhymes with *ball*?" She hears the following answers: *fall, tall, ball,* and *box*. From the children's answers she knows that at least some of them define rhyme as the same beginning sound. Her original definition of rhyming, "sounds the same," has led to some misunderstanding. She then modifies the definition so that children know what is essential. By detecting what the child is thinking, the teacher can begin to reconstruct the child's meaning.

4. *Decide how much support should be given.* Because the amount of support a child needs depends on her ZPD, children equally unable to perform a certain task may need different supports. Lisa and Fred both have trouble sounding out the word *balloon*. Lisa requires only the first sound to be able to say the word. Fred needs to have each syllable said slowly in a slurred manner before he can pronounce *balloon*. In deciding how to support a child's learning, ask questions like these: Should I vary the amount of support given to a particular child? Does the child need more verbal cues or does she need manipulatives? Do I need to change the context and try the activity in a smaller group (or larger group)? Do I need to have the child draw or represent his thinking or tell somebody else how he did it? Does this child need several cues or just one?

5. *Generate a number of possible ways of handing over the responsibility for learning to the child.* Have in mind a number of ways that you will provide scaffolding and then withdraw support in a gradual way. Keep track of the child's reaction to your hints and clues, as well as the way the child responds as you withdraw support. These will give you clues as to what works.

6. *Plan the size of the groups you will work with so that the educational dialogue is meaningful and effective.* Organize your classroom so that you have time to work with children individually and in small groups of up to 8 children. Although you can have a dialogue with the entire class, some children will dominate in larger groups. These will usually be the children at the upper and lower ends of the learning continuum. To maximize the number of dialogues you can have, use peers and prepared materials to provide scaffolding and assistance to other students at those times when you want to interact with just part of the class.

Teachers as the Planners

Teachers also engage in shared activity indirectly by modifying and planning the learning environment. By choosing manipulatives, objects, books, videos, computer programs, audiotapes, and play props, the teacher provides assistance to support independent performance. These supports are withdrawn as the child masters the skill. For example, when the child can solve a particular math problem with manipulatives, the next step is to have him draw or write, and then to solve the problem in the mind. (Of course, for some concepts it will take longer than a school year for a child to progress through all the steps.) The goal of using manipulatives is not just to solve the math problem but to provide a stepping-stone toward internalization of the concept of "number." Thus the teacher needs to plan not only how to use these aids but also how the child will make the transition from using them to more advanced forms of thinking. The use of materials is also very helpful in consolidating learning, when the child is at the independent level of the ZPD. Confirming your understanding helps the child become confident and strengthens understanding.

Teachers also orchestrate the activities shared by others in the classroom, primarily peers. We engage in teaching not only when we directly interact with children but also when we organize different peer activities to encourage learning. In the next section, we discuss the many ways peers can support each other's learning.

The Role of Peers in Shared Activity

Just interacting with another peer is not sufficient to promote a child's development. Sometimes casual interaction does help children to learn, but this learning can be haphazard, and children can be misled by each other's misunderstandings. Important attributes or concepts may not emerge in peer interaction. When children interact with each other, the social situation is full of many complex pieces of information, relating to friendships, past interactions, the content, and the goal of the group. It is very difficult for children to figure out on their own what the group is trying to accomplish in different social situations. However, by structuring the situation, the teacher can use peer interaction to further learning goals. Both the goal of the group and the type of interaction that will occur must be carefully spelled out.

In the early stages of the learning process, interaction with the teacher may be more beneficial than sharing activities with peers. This is particularly true when the child has not used a skill or strategy correctly or when a concept is still very vague. If the misunderstandings of others would confuse the child, then this is not the time for peer interaction. Cassie is just learning the concept of regrouping, and she is not sure what place value is. This is not the time for her to interact with Joseph, who is also confused and thinks that you write the *10* in the answer next to the tens place. Cassie might benefit from interacting with a more knowledgeable peer, one who is not confused; however, the teacher will probably need to clarify things for her first. Once the child has learned the skill, practice with a peer is very beneficial.

To promote learning, children must engage in very specific types of interaction with each other. Vygotskians describe the following peer interactions as the most beneficial for development.

1. *Cooperating to successfully complete a task.* Activities in which sharing is required to complete the task are more likely to lead to development. This type of activity tends to motivate children, encourages them to coordinate roles, and provides the missing components in an individual child's skills. An example is when children have complementary pieces of information and have to share and coordinate this information to solve a problem or create a whole (Cole, 1994). Each member has an essential piece of information, like a piece of a puzzle. A story is divided up into four pieces and each child is given one piece to read. The entire story line cannot be reconstructed without all of the pieces. Each child must read and summarize her own piece and present it to others in the right order. This type of cooperative activity is described by Slavin (1994) and Johnson and Johnson (1994).

2. *Assuming assigned roles.* Another way to organize the shared activity is to assign nonoverlapping roles. For example, one child draws a plan for the block building, another child builds it, and a third child checks to see whether the plan matches the final building. Each child has a distinct role, but they share the plan and the blocks. This kind of activity helps children to develop all the skills needed to complete a process: to plan, control, and monitor their behavior. Another example is a preliteracy activity for preschoolers in which the teacher assigns the roles of storyteller and listener to children in pairs. She gives the storyteller a card with a picture of a mouth and the listener a card with a picture of an ear. These cards help the children keep their roles straight.

Peer editing is another illustration of a role-based activity. In peer editing, one child writes and the other edits and checks the writer's work. When assigning a checking, directing, or editing role, it is important to be explicit about the standards for evaluating the peer's work. Do not have children just say if they like the story. Shared activity is a vehicle for children to learn concepts, skills, and strategies; these must be made explicit or the children will not learn them. The more specific you can be about what you want them to do, the better. A second-grade teacher asks editors to comment on the use of flow of the story, the main character, and simple grammar (use of sentences and periods). To support children in playing the role of editor the teacher has them put on their "editor's eyes," a pair of eyeglasses without lenses, or use a magnifying glass. By taking the role of editor, the child will appropriate the ideas of flow, character, and grammar as the child regulates his partner. This type of activity uses the principle that other-regulation precedes self-regulation.

3. *Acting as sounding board for a peer.* Children can be paired to help each other think through a problem, thus promoting thinking while talking (see Chapter 8). Thinking while talking helps children to externalize their internal, folded thinking. By explaining things back and forth, they clarify their own thinking. An illustration of the peer as sounding board is the author's chair or reading buddy activity, when children read their own stories aloud. Reading aloud makes the child think while talking. Children will add new information as they read aloud and hear their own inconsistencies. As peers respond to the reading, the author begins to understand what is unclear to others. By summarizing the questions the peers ask, teachers can help the author to begin to learn how to self-question. Using a tape recorder can also help the child to revisit and reexamine his thinking. The peers are the social context that makes the reading aloud meaningful to the child.

4. *Acting for an imaginary person.* Preparing something for an imaginary character or for someone who is not physically present, such as a sick peer or a grandparent who lives far away, creates a shared learning situation, too. This type of activity provokes the same kind of decontextualized thinking that forces children to provide more explicit and elaborate explanations. Drawing a map for a newcomer to campus leads kindergartners to produce highly detailed maps of the school campus. Reading to a stuffed animal prompts the same kinds of reading behavior as reading to a real person. In another example, a preschool teacher who had a hamster in her class encouraged more detailed dictated stories after the teacher-as-hamster wrote the children a "letter".

5. *Acting as the expert or the novice.* When a peer expert helps a novice, or gives peer tutoring, there are double benefits for learning. First, peer tutoring helps the novice, who is at the lower level of understanding, by providing individualized support. Second, it helps the expert by requiring that child to be more explicit and consistent. It supports the learning of metacognitive skills for the expert as well as a deeper understanding of content (Cohen, Kulik, & Kulik, 1982).

To make peer tutoring work in the early childhood setting, the activity must be carefully planned. The tutor needs extensive training about how to help another person to learn. The young expert is likely to tell the answer rather than model strategies, which is not helpful for the novice. Show the expert exactly how to act: what to do if the answer is partly correct or wrong, and how to praise and encourage the other child. If a child never gets the chance to be an expert, then this kind of pairing can be very discouraging. Make sure that every child gets a chance to be the expert. Pair lower-functioning children with children in a lower grade; for example, first graders can read a familiar book to preschoolers or kindergartners who cannot read.

6. *Playing.* Another way that teachers can plan to use peers is to initiate a game or to facilitate dramatic play. For more information, see Chapter 10.

7. *Creating cognitive conflict.* Sometimes children in a group will have different opinions or perspectives. A natural outgrowth of these disagreements is cognitive conflict which can be conducive to growth. Both Piagetians and Vygotskians believe that encountering incompatible or different views of the same situation improves the individual child's ability to experiment mentally. For example, 8-year-old Donna learns that the earth revolves around the sun, and in a discussion she finds out that other children believe the sun revolves around the earth. Until she has to explain her ideas to another child, she will not understand the internal logic of her own belief or the conclusions that this would lead to. In older children, this external discussion can occur internally.

As we can see, children benefit from all types of shared activities, with adults, peers, and materials. Ways of implementing shared activities in specific activities will be discussed in Section IV.

For Further Reading

Newman D., Griffin P., & Cole, M. (1989). *The construction zone: Working for cognitive change in school.* Cambridge: Cambridge University Press.

Rogoff, B. (1990). *Apprenticeship in thinking: Cognitive development in social context.* New York: Oxford University Press.

Rubtsov, V. V. (1991). *Learning in children: Organization and development of cooperative actions.* New York: Nova Science Publishers.

Applying the Vygotskian Approach in the Classroom

In this section we describe how to apply the Vygotskian approach in the early childhood classroom. The strategies and tactics for learning/teaching are once again presented but this time in the context of actual activities teachers can use in their classrooms. We devote a chapter specifically to play because it is the leading activity for the early childhood period. The final chapter provides a number of different kinds of activities including some appropriate for children up through second grade.

Chapter 10   Play as a Leading Activity

Chapter 11   Activities for the Early Childhood Classroom

Play as a Leading Activity

Joseph enters the housekeeping area. He grabs a spoon, pretends to eat, puts the spoon down, and walks to the cupboard. He opens the cupboard and looks inside. He opens and shuts the door several times. He looks at two other children who are talking as they sit together pretending to eat a meal. Joseph leans up against their table and shoves a plate back and forth. He then goes to the dress-up carton and looks at the shoes. He puts two pairs in a row and then walks to the block area.

Marina enters the housekeeping area. "I'm going to play that I'm the Mommy," she says to no one in particular. "I'm going to make dinner, and then I'll give the baby a bath." Jim starts to wash dishes in the sink. "No, don't," Marina says as she pushes him away. Marina opens the cupboard under the sink and looks around. She starts to wash dishes.

Matthew and Eric are in the block area. "Let's build a city," says Matthew. "We're going to need all the long blocks. You start here." Eric says, "How many houses should we make? Let's go all the way over to here with houses and a road." While building, they keep bumping into each other. Eric says, "I know what—I'll build, and you can bring me the blocks, 'cuz there isn't any room. I'll tell you which ones I need. Bring me a really long one." Matthew makes crane noises and movements, picking up the block in his hand and lowering it: "Vroom. . .ting, ting, ting. I'm lowering the block."

These are three examples of play in any early childhood classroom. How you interpret these vignettes depends on your beliefs about play and its significance in child behavior. In this chapter we discuss different ways of interpreting a child's play behavior and the Vygotskian perspective on play.

Definitions of Play

The popular conception of play is that it is the opposite of work. It describes any situation in which people are not productive or doing something specific. Play is also thought of as something that is enjoyable, free, and spontaneous. This view of play, however, denies the importance of play in the development of young children.

Over the years, many psychological theorists have emphasized the importance of play in child development. They stress various aspects of play and how it influences specific psychological processes. In this section we discuss several of these theories: psychoanalysis, the social development perspective, and the constructivist approach.

The Psychoanalytic View of Play

According to Erikson (1963, 1977) and Anna Freud (1966), play substitutes for unfulfilled wishes and offers a way to relieve and relive traumatic events of the past. The psychoanalytic approach emphasizes the social-emotional side of play. Through play, the child resolves psychological conflicts with parents or irrational fears. A child who plays monsters is overcoming her fear of the dark. A little boy punishes his doll for an imagined transgression just as his parents punish him. For Erikson, play is also a way for the child to explore, to show initiative and independence; it is the stage the child is in during the preschool period. In the psychoanalytic view, play is a way to channel aggression through a cathartic experience. It is a reaction to the past and a mechanism for revisiting past events.

Play as Social Development

Parten (1932) and a number of other theorists (Howes, 1980; Rubin, 1980) view play as a form of social interaction that facilitates and mirrors the child's growing ability to engage in cooperative actions with peers. The early stages of play are marked by little or no direct interaction with peers and an inability to use social skills in play. Later stages are marked by the ability to take another's perspective, coordination of different roles (e.g., one mommy, one baby), discussion about the content of play, and negotiation of disputes. Dramatic and pretend situations are commonly considered more mature types of play interactions. Some researchers have examined rough-and-tumble play as social play. Rough-and-tumble play encompasses all of the wrestling and chase-type play that appears at the end of the preschool period. Like social play, rough-and-tumble play involves roles.

Constructivist Theories About Play

According to Piaget (1945/1962), play performs a major role in the child's growing mental abilities. Piaget describes several stages in the development of play. The first stage, called *practice* or *functional play,* is a characteristic of the sensorimotor period. During functional play the child repeats known schemes for actions and using objects. For example, the child "drinks" from an empty cup or pretends to brush his hair with his hand.

Symbolic play, the second stage, emerges during the preoperational period. It involves the use of mental representations in which objects stand for other objects. In symbolic play, a block could be a telephone, a boat, a banana, a dog, or a spaceship. Piaget made a distinction between constructive and dramatic play. In constructive play, concrete objects are used to build and create other objects. For example, a set of wooden blocks might be used to build a city for toy cars and trucks. In dramatic play, children create pretend situations and roles using gesture and language. They create and negotiate what role each child will play and come up with a theme or direction for an imaginary scenario. Dramatic play usually surfaces slightly behind the emergence of constructive play. Piaget (1945/1962) saw the pretend nature of play during this period as a reflection of the child's egocentric thought. Symbolic play, according to Piaget, disappears at the beginning of the concrete operational period, around 7 years of age.

The final stage of play is *games with rules* which peaks during the concrete operational period. This stage is marked by the use of external rules to initiate, regulate, maintain, and terminate social interaction. Some rules are formal, set and handed down by others, and other rules are generated and negotiated during the play, as children invent the game as they play.

Several contemporary researchers have extended Piaget's ideas of play. Smilansky and Shefatya (1990) confirmed that the emergence of play directly correlates with the development of language, problem solving, and logical mathematical thinking. However, Smilansky and Shefatya disagree with Piaget's idea that play is a natural outgrowth of the progression from the sensorimotor stage to preoperations to concrete operations. They argue that the development of play depends on the social context and adult guidance. They also argue that play training is necessary for some children and showed through their research that adults can successfully increase children's level of play. This increased level of play had a positive effect on the other cognitive skills.

Play in the Vygotskian Framework

Vygotsky believed that play promotes cognitive, emotional, and social development. Unlike the other theorists discussed above, Vygotsky had a more integrated view of the value of play in development.

For Vygotsky, play serves as a tool of the mind enabling children to master their own behavior (Vygotsky, 1966/1977). The imaginary situations created in play are the first constraints that channel and direct behavior in a specific way. Play organizes behavior. Instead of producing totally spontaneous behavior, in play the child acts like a mommy or like a truck driver, for example.

Each imaginary situation contains a set of roles and rules which surface naturally. Roles are the characters that the children play, such as pirate or teacher. Rules are the set of behaviors allowed either by the role or by the pretend scenario. The roles and rules change as the theme for the imaginary situation changes. For instance, a group of children playing grocery store will have different roles from another group that is playing at being a pride of lions. At first the rules are hidden in the play; later, these rules become explicit and are negotiated between children.

Play, then, involves an explicit imaginary situation and hidden or implicit rules. The imaginary situation is the pretend situation that children create. Although the situation is imaginary, it can be seen by others because children make the characteristics of the situation explicit. They say, "Let's pretend there is a chair here and a table here. We'll pretend there are six children in our class and we are the teachers." Children can also make the situation explicit using gestures and noises, such as "vroom, vroom" as a truck pulls out of a gas station or "neiheyheyhey" as the child pulls on the reins of an imaginary horse.

Rules, on the other hand, are considered implicit because they cannot be seen easily and can only be inferred from behavior. Rules are expressed as the pattern of behavior that is associated with a specific role. Each role in an imaginary play situation imposes its own rules on the child's behavior. From a Western perspective, this is a very unusual way to think of play, since we traditionally view play as totally spontaneous and free of any constraints.

Vygotsky, however, argues that in play children do not merely act any way they please; they follow specific rules for behavior. Children distinguish between playing mommy and playing teacher. There are different gestures, costumes, and even language that go with each role. Children at the early stages of play will not be aware of these differences. However, most 4 year olds show that they are sensitive to mistakes in the carrying out of a role and often correct each other: "Mommies carry a briefcase!" "When you're the teacher, the children have to sit down." "The teacher reads the book this way." Children even enjoy violating the rules of the role as a joke. Three-year-old Toby says, "Now I'm the Daddy," as he climbs into his high chair and then bursts out laughing, "Daddy can't sit in the high chair!"

How Play Influences Development

Recent Western research summarized by Smilansky and Shefatya (1990) indicates that growth in dramatic play leads to gains in cognitive and social development as well as school-related skills. Examples include growth in "verbalization, vocabulary, language comprehension, attention span, imaginativeness, concentration, impulse control, curiosity, more problem solving strategies, cooperation, empathy, and group participation" (Smilansky & Shefatya, 1990, p. 220).

Vygotskians have examined the mechanisms by which play influences development. For example, Manujlenko (Elkonin, 1978) and Istomina (1948/1977) found that the child's mental skills are at a higher level during play than in other learning activities, representing what Vygotsky identified as the higher level of the ZPD. Manujlenko found higher levels of self-regulation during play than during other times of the day. When a boy was asked to be the lookout, he remained at his post and concentrated for a longer period of time than he could at times when the teacher asked him to pay attention to something. Istomina compared the number of items children could remember deliberately during dramatic play involving a grocery store and under conditions similar to a typical laboratory experiment. Children were given a list of words to remember. In the dramatic play situation, children were given the list as they played grocery store. In the laboratory experiment condition, the children were given the list on a piece of paper. Manujlenko found that children could remember more items in the dramatic play condition.

Vygotskians argue that play influences development in three ways:

1. Play creates the child's zone of proximal development.
2. Play facilitates the separation of thought from actions and objects.
3. Play facilitates the development of self-regulation.

Creating the Zone of Proximal Development
For Vygotsky, play establishes a zone of proximal development for the child:

> Play also creates the zone of proximal development of the child. In play the child is always behaving beyond his age, above his usual everyday behavior; in play he is, as it were, a head above himself. Play contains in a concentrated form, as in the focus of a magnifying glass, all developmental tendencies; it is as if the child tries to jump above his usual level. The relationship of play to development should be compared to the relationship between instruction and development. . . . Play is a source of development and creates the zone of proximal development. (Vygotsky, 1933/1978, p. 74).

It is not just the content of the play that defines the ZPD. The psychological processes that the child must engage in, in order to play, create the ZPD. The roles, rules, and motivational support provided by the imaginary situation provide the assistance necessary for the child to perform at a higher level of his ZPD.

If we compare the child's behavior in play and nonplay settings, we see the higher and lower levels of the ZPD. In the nonplay, or real-life, situation in a grocery store, Louis wants candy, but his mother won't give it to him so he cries. He cannot control his behavior. He reacts automatically to wanting candy and even says, "I can't stop crying." While playing, Louis *can* control his behavior, because he controls the imaginary situation of the family. He can pretend to go to the grocery store and not cry. He can pretend to cry and then make himself stop. Play allows him to act at a higher level than he can when he is in the actual situation.

In a classroom example, Jessica, a 5 year old, has trouble sitting at group circle time. She leans on other children and talks to her neighbor. In spite of the teacher's verbal cues and support, she cannot sit for more than 3 minutes. In contrast, when she is playing school with several of her friends, she can sit during the pretend group circle time. Pretending to be a good student, she can concentrate and act interested for 10 minutes. Thus, play provides the roles, rules, and scenario that enable her to focus and attend at a higher level than she performs without this scaffolding.

If a child has no experience in play, we expect that both cognitive and social-emotional development will suffer. This idea was refined by Vygotsky's students Leont'ev (1977/1978) and Elkonin (1971/1977) into the idea of play as a leading activity (see Chapters 5 and 6). They state that play is the most important activity for development for children age 3 to 6. Leont'ev and Elkonin believed that for this age group play has a unique role and cannot be replaced by any other activity, even though children benefit from a variety of experiences during this period. Their research on play as a leading activity will be discussed later in this chapter.

By the "focus of a magnifying glass" Vygotsky meant that new developmental accomplishments become apparent in play far earlier that they do in other activities, especially learning activities. Thus, at age 4 academic-type activities, such as recognizing letters, are not as good as play at predicting later abilities to learn. In a 4-year-old's play we can observe the abilities of attention, symbolizing, and problem solving at a higher level. We are actually watching the child of tomorrow.

Separating Thought from Actions and Objects

In play, children act in accordance with internal ideas rather than external reality:

> The child sees one thing, but acts differently in relation to what he sees. Thus a condition is reached in which the child begins to act independently of what he sees. (Vygotsky, 1933/1978, p. 97)

Because play requires the substitution of one object for another, the child begins to separate the meaning or idea of the object from the object itself (Berk, 1994). When the child uses a block as a boat, the idea of "boatness" becomes separated from the actual boat. If the block is made to act like a boat, then it can stand for that boat. As preschoolers grow, their ability to make these substitutions becomes more flexible. Eventually objects can be symbolized by a simple gesture or by saying "Let's pretend. . . ."

This separation of the meaning from the object is preparation for the development of abstract ideas and abstract thinking (Berk, 1994). In abstract thinking we evaluate, manipulate, and monitor thoughts and ideas without reference to the real world. This act of separating object and idea is also preparation for the transition to writing, where the word looks nothing like the object it stands for. Finally, behavior is no longer driven by the object; it is no longer reactive. Objects can be used as tools to understand other ideas. Instead of using the block as a block, the child can use it to solve problems, as in using them as math manipulatives.

Developing Self-Regulation

Because play requires that children inhibit and restrain their behavior according to the roles and rules of the particular play theme, play helps children practice self-regulation. In play children cannot act any way they please; they must act in a way that conforms to the play scenario. Louis, who is 2 ½, is playing family and cries like the baby. The role of baby implies that he must pretend to cry and stop when the father comforts him. His behavior is initiated by the play situation and is not a reaction to being hurt. This act (of crying) requires the same deliberateness used in higher mental functions. Thus play provides the context in which Louis can practice deliberate behavior; it shows that he can master his behavior. Play requires significantly more control and deliberateness than other contexts. Thus it provides a ZPD for the development of higher mental functions.

The Developmental Path of Play

Among all of Vygotsky's students, it was Elkonin (1969, 1971, 1977, 1978) who focused his research on play. Elkonin did research and tried interventions to show the connection between play and the development of learning activities in older children. He elaborated on Leont'ev's concept of leading activity and identified the properties that make play a leading activity. In this section we present the description of play derived from his research.

Play in Toddlers

According to Elkonin (1969, 1978), the roots of play lie in the manipulative or instrumental activities of toddlers, age 1 to about 3. During manipulative activities, children explore the properties of objects and learn to use them in a conventional way. Then, as children begin to use everyday objects in imaginary situations, play emerges. For example, 2-year-old Leila picks up a spoon and tries to feed herself. She uses the spoon in a conventional way, not just to bang on the table. The first signs of play occur when 18-month-old John "feeds" his bear or pretends to feed himself. Play springs out of the child's exploration and use of common everyday objects.

For the behavior to become play, the child must label the action with words. Thus, language plays an important role in transforming behavior from manipulation into play. When the teacher says, "Will you feed your bear?" he helps the toddler who has just picked up a spoon to make the transition to play. Twenty-month-old Jody rolls the toy truck back and listens to the sounds it makes. Her teacher says, "Why don't you drive your truck over here and give it some gas?" Jody responds and drives her truck over to the teacher, who pretends to put some gas in it. Without the teacher's language and interaction, Jody would only continue to listen to the sounds of the wheels and explore the movement of the truck. The teacher's actions create a ZPD, pushing the child to a more sophisticated level, from manipulation to play.

Now the child can pretend to be somebody else or use an object in a symbolic way. Like Piaget, Elkonin defined *symbolic function* as using an object to represent something else. To qualify as play, exploration of objects must include symbolic representation. When a child squeezes, drops, and bangs an object on the table, this is object manipulation, not play. Only when the child uses the object as a duck and makes it swim on the table and peck bread crumbs would the actions become play.

Play in Preschoolers and Kindergartners

Elkonin (1971, 1977, 1978) describes play in preschool years as initially *object-oriented*. This play focuses on objects, while the roles of the players in the interaction are of secondary importance. When 3-year-old Joann and Tomaso play house together, they say to each other, "We're playing house," but the roles of adults in the family are not enacted. They spend their time washing dishes and stirring pots on the stove, and they do not talk to each other very much.

Contrast this with the play of older preschoolers and kindergartners which is much more socially oriented. For 5-year-old children, stirring the pots and washing dishes provide a context for the intricate social roles they enact. The objects are not the focus of play. The actions of washing and stirring can even be abbreviated or just labeled verbally. In socially oriented play, roles are negotiated and enacted for an extended period of time. The child becomes the character she is playing. This kind of play is typical for children between the ages of 4 and 6, but continues in some forms through elementary school.

In the Vygotskian paradigm, socially oriented play does not have to occur with other children. The child can engage in what is called *director's play,* when children play with pretend playmates or direct and act out a scene with toys. Isaac pretends to be the conductor of a symphony orchestra made up of stuffed animals and dolls. Maya plays school, pretending at one moment to be the teacher and at another talking for her teddy bear student. Unlike some Western researchers (e.g., Parten, 1932), Vygotskians do not consider all solitary play immature. If the child is playing alone but pretending that there are other people, then director's play is considered the equivalent of social pretend play.

In contrast to Piaget (1945/1951), Vygotskians do not believe that socially oriented play disappears when children reach the age of 7 or 8. Children at 10 and 11 still play socially, but the importance of social play as a leading activity dies away. As children get older, they develop more explicit rules for their socially oriented play. Six-year-old Frank says, "This one will be the bad guy, and bad guys always try to capture the good guy." Mary replies, "OK, but he won't be able to because good guys are faster and their planes are better, so they'll get away." The older the child, the more time is spent in negotiating roles and actions (rules) and the less time is spent on acting out the script (imaginary situation). In fact, 6 year olds often spend several minutes discussing a scenario and only a few seconds acting out the situation.

Games

Games are another type of play that emerges at around 5 years of age. Games are distinguished from imaginary play by the fact that the imaginary situation is hidden and the rules are explicit and detailed:

> For example, playing chess creates an imaginary situation. Why? Because the knight, king, queen, and so forth can only move in a specified way; because covering and taking pieces are purely chess concepts. Although in the chess game there is no direct substitute for real-life relationships, it is a kind of imaginary situation nevertheless. (Vygotsky, 1933/1978, p. 95)

Another example is soccer, a game in which players are not allowed to touch the ball with their hands. Soccer is an imaginary situation, since in reality all of the players could use their hands to move the ball. However, all of the players agree that they will not use their hands. This situation is similar to children spelling out what they can or cannot do during dramatic play.

Games are distinguished from socially oriented play by the balance between roles and rules. In socially oriented play, the roles are explicit and the rules are not. Children discuss the roles and what is expected, but breaking the rules does not disrupt social play. A child can do something out of the agreed-upon sequence, but this will not upset the play. In contrast, games have explicit rules; if the rules are broken, then the game cannot continue.

Play as a Leading Activity

Not all play can be considered a leading activity because not all playlike behaviors promote development. The following are the major characteristics of play that prepare the child for later learning activity:

1. Symbolic representations and symbolic actions
2. Complex interwoven themes
3. Complex interwoven roles
4. Extended time frame (over several days)

While some of these characteristics are just emerging in the play of 3 year olds, all of them should be present by the time children leave kindergarten.

1. *Symbolic representations and symbolic actions.* In advanced play, children use objects and actions symbolically, to represent other objects and actions. Children who play at this level do not discontinue their play if they do not have the exact toy or prop. They merely invent or substitute something else. They may even

agree to pretend to have the object and not require a physical substitute. Children at this level treat actions symbolically too. They may agree that the building has fallen down and do not need to make the structure fall. They only need to say, "Let's pretend it fell down." Settings that evoke this kind of inventiveness will promote more play.

2. *Complex interwoven themes.* Advanced play has multiple themes that are interwoven to make a whole. Children easily incorporate new people, toys, and ideas without disrupting the flow of play. Children also integrate seemingly unrelated themes into an imaginary situation. For example, they might pretend that the mechanic gets sick fixing an ambulance and has to call the doctor, thus merging a hospital theme and a garage theme.

3. *Complex interwoven roles.* In advanced play, children simultaneously assume, coordinate, and integrate many roles. In less advanced play, children enact stereotypical roles tied to one theme, such as being the mommy who feeds the baby and does dishes. Once play becomes more advanced, "Mommy" goes off to work and to the hospital with a sick child, then turns into the doctor who heals the child, next becomes the child who cries, and then returns to the original mommy role.

4. *Extended time frame.* The extended time frame of advanced play refers to two different aspects of play. First, it refers to how long the child can sustain the play. The longer a child maintains different roles, the more advanced the play. Second, it refers to whether or not the play lasts longer than one day. Older children typically continue the same "battle" or "hospital" for several consecutive days. With assistance, even 4 year olds can sustain play for several days. Most early childhood teachers do not consider extending play for several days because they are usually thinking in terms of a single day's play session. According to Vygotsky and Elkonin, continued play pushes children to the highest level of their ZPD by requiring more self-regulation, planning, and memory.

Enriching Play

When we recommend that teachers assist in play, we do not mean that teachers should play with children or direct play as a member of the group. Remember that the child must be active and motivated to engage in play. Children play for different reasons than they interact with adults. Interaction with an adult places the child in a very specific, subordinate role, and no matter what the teacher does, the child is still a child. Children in play take on various roles and try them out. If a teacher takes too much of a lead in play, children never get a chance to see what it is like to pretend.

Another disadvantage of too much adult direction is that the teacher will not be able to glimpse what lies within each child's ZPD. The teacher's actions will tend to expose a specific side of the child. Only by stepping back and watching the child interact with peers can the teacher see the child's potential in a different social context. This other social context may show a side of the child the teacher would never otherwise know.

Teachers, nonetheless, play an important role in assisting the play process. Sensitive teachers who provide appropriate scaffolding have a positive impact on the level of play in their classrooms (Berk, 1994; Smilansky & Shefatya, 1990). Teachers can do the following to assist play:

1. Make sure children have sufficient time for play.
2. Help children plan their play.
3. Monitor the progress of play.
4. Choose appropriate props and toys.
5. Provide themes that can be extended from one day to the next.
6. Coach individuals who need help.
7. Suggest or model how themes can be woven together.
8. Model appropriate ways to solve disputes.

1. *Make sure children have sufficient time for play.* Young preschool children and toddlers need time to interact over objects with adults nearby for guidance and help with social conflicts. Children at this age may need more adult guidance than older preschool children. Teachers will need to plan sufficient time for play that can occur when they are able to watch and coax interaction along when necessary.

Older preschool-age children need a substantial block of time to develop the themes and roles of rich social play. They need time each day, so that themes can be carried over from one day to the next. Teachers should make sure there is enough time allotted during the day, at least 30-40 minutes, for uninterrupted play.

The issue of play is also important in kindergarten and first and second grade. One of the negative outcomes of mixed-age grouping can be that kindergarten children, who would usually be given time for play during the school day, are given less time for this type of interaction. Play in the early primary grades is not part of the daily schedule but is expected to occur during recess. We believe that play is very important in the early school years. Time should be allotted for play outside of recess, or recess time should be extended so that play can develop.

2. *Help children plan their play.* Before play begins, ask children what they plan to do. Although the children do not have to follow the specific plan, verbalizing ideas promotes better understanding and establishes the state of shared activity. Encourage children to discuss their play. Help them identify new props or roles.

The best time to help children plan their play is right before the children begin playing. In some programs, a planning time at the beginning of the day is used to describe what will be done. Because most children in preschool do not have deliberate memory, they may find it difficult to remember what they decided to do several hours earlier. If they do not have a reminder of the plan right before they begin, they will not make the connection between planning and action. Many programs have children recap their experiences at the end of the day only; this is not sufficient to prompt the appropriate connection. When they are reminded of their plan at the end of the day, they may not remember what they did. If you have a morning planning time, you will still need to prompt the memory of the plan right before the children begin.

As playtime ends, ask the children if they want to continue tomorrow, and encourage them to figure out what they need to put aside for tomorrow. This strategy extends the play for more than one day. Begin the play the next day by going over the previous day's plans and activities.

Remember that sticking to the plan is not a goal in itself. It is just a means of helping children see continuity in their actions.

3. *Monitor the progress of play.* Watch what the children do as they play. Think about the characteristics of mature play and what you might suggest to develop their skills during the play period. It is important not to be too intrusive or to make too many suggestions.

You should model how to verbally describe what children are doing at the beginning of the play period. For example you can say, "Are you the vet or are you the patient?" or "I see Marty is going to work."

4. *Choose appropriate props and toys.* According to Vygotsky, the teacher should stock the play area with toys and props that have multiple functions. For example, several large pieces of colorful cloth would be better than a specific "princess" dress. Use toys from different cultures. When children cannot find exactly the prop they want, encourage them to make one up. They might use another object, like a block, or they can just pretend they have the object.

5. *Provide themes that can be extended from one day to the next.* Use stories, field trips, activities in the classroom, or child-generated ideas, to find themes for play. For example, a child might pretend to be an artist after drawing pictures in art. At the beginning, children may need support in remembering the roles and events that took place. However, once assisted, children are usually able to continue on their own.

6. *Coach individuals who may need help.* Watch for children who avoid the play area. These children may need support in joining the group, accepting new ideas, or including new partners.

Look at the child's level of play. If he is primarily just playing with objects, then providing support at the next developmental level will be beneficial. The teacher can help this child by adding the imaginary context that the child is not yet verbalizing. A teacher can ask a child who is making mudpies, "Are you making mudpies for a party or are you going to sell them in the store?" Sometimes this is enough to trigger imaginary play.

7. *Suggest or model how themes can be woven together.* Read and act out stories with different variations of a single theme. For example, read stories about bears in the zoo and bears in the wild to discover how the same bear theme can change. You can play a "what if" game to combine themes that seem different but can be merged. For example, if Mara wants to play school and Tony wants to play cars, the teacher can suggest, "What if Mara's class wants to go on a field trip, how could Tony help her?"

8. *Model appropriate ways to solve disputes.* In play, children learn how to solve social disputes. Teachers cannot expect them to always be able to work out these

problems alone. Children with poor social skills need additional assistance. Teachers can model ways of talking that will help children work through disagreements, such as "I feel _____." "I don't like it when _____," or "What if we _____ instead of _____?" Using external mediators, as discussed in Chapter 7, is also helpful. One teacher keeps a "dispute bag" containing a coin, dice, straws of different lengths, a dreidel, a spinner, and cards with rhymes on them (such as "One potato, two potato . . .") to help children solve disagreements.

For Further Reading

Berk, L. E. (1994). Vygotsky's theory: The importance of make-believe play. *Young Children, 50*(1), 30-39.

Berk, L. E., & Winsler, A. (1995). Scaffolding children's learning: Vygotsky and early childhood education. *NAEYC Research and Practice Series, 7.* Washington, DC: National Association for the Education of Young Children.

Elkonin, D. (1977). Toward the problem of stages in the mental development of the child. In M. Cole (Ed.), *Soviet developmental psychology.* White Plains, NY: M. E. Sharpe. (Original work published in 1971)

Newman F., & Holzman L. (1993). *Lev Vygotsky: Revolutionary scientist.* New York: Routledge.

Vygotsky, L. S. (1977). Play and its role in the mental development of the child. In J. S. Bruner, A. Jolly, & K. Sylva (Eds.), *Play: Its role in development and evolution* (pp. 537–554). New York: Basic Books. (Original work published in 1966)

CHAPTER 11

Activities for the Early Childhood Classroom

This chapter provides examples of how the Vygotskian framework may be applied to activities in the early childhood classroom. In a short book, it is not possible to outline an entire Vygotskian-based curriculum. However, it is possible to help you view some typical classroom activities in a different light. We encourage you to try out some of the activities from this new slant and note how the results are similar to or different from what usually happens. After trying the activities out, you can begin to modify them to fit your own needs.

Vygotskians believe that activities in all types of contexts are necessary for development—including large-muscle activities, activities with math manipulatives, social interactions, dramatic play, and circle time or group meetings—and that teachers need to carefully note which contexts work best for different children. In some of the following activities we describe the levels of maximum assistance and minimum assistance needed to foster independent performance. Our aim is to help teachers think through how to hand over responsibility to the children. The development of self-regulation and independent performance is the overarching goal of all activities.

The activities are described by the age of the children for whom they are appropriate and the types of learning they promote. They have been adapted from activities used in Russian classrooms and pilot-tested in 10 elementary schools in Denver, Colorado. The classrooms used to develop these activities included preschools, kindergarten, first grade, second grade, and multiage classrooms (kindergarten-first-second and first-second).

Block Building

Purpose of Activity

As a shared activity, block building fosters self-regulation, planning, and coordination of roles in younger preschool children and facilitates moving back and forth between symbolic representation (drawing) and concrete manipulation in older children. To be a shared activity, block play must include the sharing of the same structure and the use of language to discuss the joint activity. When children are building next to each other but are not talking and jointly constructing, then the block building is not considered a shared activity.

Procedure

Articulating a plan is the first step. All children are encouraged to describe what they plan to build before they begin using blocks, even though younger children will not be able to carry out a specific plan. The plan can be changed or abandoned as the building progresses and the children negotiate what they want to construct.

Block building can be set up as a shared activity with specific roles assigned by the children or suggested by the teacher. Encourage children to work on the structure together. Through this shared building, children learn to regulate each other, be regulated themselves, and to talk about their ideas. Once the cooperative nature of block building has been established, teachers foster further development of cognitive skills by having children build a structure that will meet certain external criteria, such as "big enough for a toy elephant" or "large enough to be a home for six animals." This type of building requires an even higher level of planning and coregulation.

In addition, block building can be set up to alternate between representational drawing and concrete manipulation. By moving back and forth between these two types of activity, children strengthen the connections between them and move to higher levels of abstraction and planning. Children as young as 3 years of age can plan their structures on paper with the use of colored pieces of paper in the shape of the blocks (see Figure 11.1). Once they have made a plan, they build it themselves or have another classmate build it. Then they can compare the real structure to the plan. Children 5 to 8 years of age can use templates, their own drawings, or a computer program to generate the plan. With older children, the buildings will become more complicated, and sophisticated roles can be assigned, such as architect, builder, and building inspector.

Materials.   You will need construction blocks, construction-paper shapes that will stand for blocks, templates, and paper.

Figure 11.1.   Child using paper cutouts for building

Evaluating Learning

1. Is there growth in the child's ability to articulate a plan? How detailed is it?
2. Is there growth in the child's ability to participate in a shared activity in which the children cooperate to plan the structure's characteristics and negotiate their roles? How much teacher support is necessary to sustain a 5-minute interaction?
3. Is there growth in the complexity of the structures the child plans on paper?
4. Is there growth in the child's ability to take on different roles in planning, carrying out the plan, and checking the plan? How much support from the teacher is necessary to sustain a 5-minute interaction?

Mapping

Purpose of Activity

Maps and plans promote symbolic thinking and extend the child's repertoire of "languages" and external mediators. Maps and plans can be incorporated in many activities, making them more deliberate and structured.

Procedure

At the beginning, maps and plans should be very simple and introduced in a familiar context. For example, children playing might make a plan to rearrange the furniture in their classroom or a dollhouse (see Figure 11.2). If children cannot draw well enough, they can use paper squares and circles to stand for pieces of furniture. After making a simple plan, the furniture should be rearranged, even if only temporarily, because it is important for children to compare the final outcome to their initial plan.

Older children can use plans and maps in games such as Treasure Hunt (see Figure 11.3) as well as in real-life situations, such as making a map for visitors to the school. At this point, teachers should introduce conventional symbols used in maps, such as the points of the compass (N, S, W, E).

Keep in mind the following when designing activities with plans:

1. Create a map to represent a real situation, such as a plan of a room or a map of a neighborhood.
2. Change the arrangement of objects (or tell children about these changes) and let children adjust their maps accordingly. For example, younger children can rearrange toy furniture in a dollhouse and then create a new plan that reflects the changes. Older children can draw a map of a familiar street after new houses are built.
3. Change the map and let children alter (or describe verbally) the new arrangement of objects. For example, you might change the original map of a park to show how equipment has been moved around on the playground.
4. Let several children identify different routes on a map. For example, two children can be given maps of a school building to use to navigate their way to a specific place. Both of them will meet at the library, but one child will start from the principal's office and the other from the cafeteria.

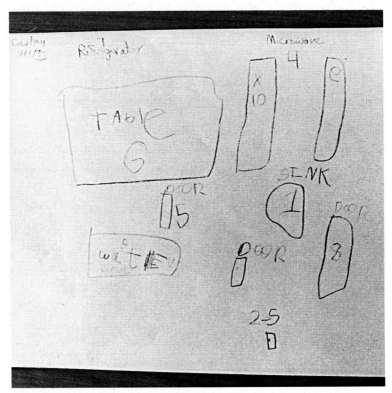

Figure 11.2.   Plan of preschool room

5. Have two children create maps for each other and then follow specific directions using the partner's map. A variation of this activity involves not only following the map but also following the directions left at each stop along the way. Children follow the map to the first stop. There they find a note with directions such as "Take a marble from the basket," "Jump up and down three times," or "What is the name of the animal on the desk?" After the children solve the problem or follow the directions, they can move on to the next site on the map.

Materials.   To have children practice using ready-made maps and plans, you will need maps, plans, and a compass. To have children construct their own maps, you will need paper, pencils, rulers, and templates or construction paper for cutting out items to be placed on the map.

Evaluating Learning

1. How accurate is a child in representing the spatial relationships of objects on a map? Remember, it is not necessary for the objects themselves to be drawn accurately, but the placement on the map relative to other objects is important.

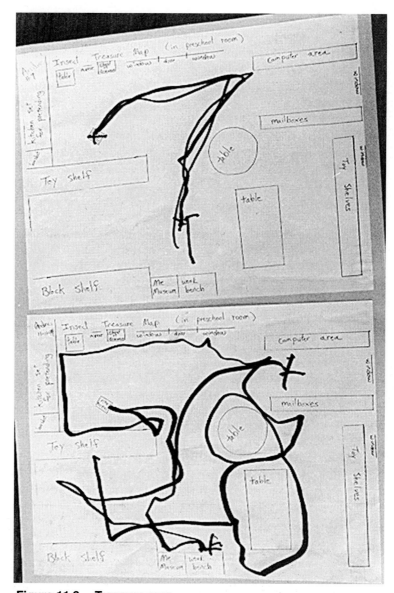

Figure 11.3.   Treasure map

2. Is there growth in the child's ability to use symbols to relate a real place to a map or plan of it? Does the child need to manipulate real objects before changing the plan or can she do it mentally?

3. Is there growth in the child's ability to use symbols to communicate with others? Is there a transition from child-generated symbols to conventional ones?

4. Is there growth in the complexity of the child's maps and plans? Can the child alter a map or plan according to perspectives of different persons viewing the situation from different points?

Making Patterns

Purpose of Activity

Pattern making not only develops children's ability to understand underlying relationships between objects but also provides practice in using symbols to represent these relationships. Children should be exposed to many different kinds of patterns, such as block patterns; rhymes and other kinds of word patterns; melodies, rhythms, and other musical patterns; and patterns in movement.

In the beginning, children are able to identify only simple patterns that are primarily teacher-demonstrated. They may not be able to identify patterns in everyday life, such as rows of vegetables in a garden or place settings at snack time. As children learn more about patterns, their understanding will become more general, transcending any specific context. Teachers should not limit children's exposure to patterns to math activities. Children will benefit from multiple experiences in making and identifying patterns in reading, building, drawing, and even cooking.

Use simple repeating patterns (AB AB AB) for younger children, and as these are mastered add more difficult patterns. Difficult patterns have more items (ABC ABC ABC), repetitions within items (AABC AABC or ABBBC ABBBC), or growing patterns (ABC AABBCC AAABBBCCC), as shown in Figure 11.4. Understanding patterns is one of the national math standards for young children (National Council of Teachers of Mathematics, 1989)

Procedure

To make greater use of pattern activities that are already being used in the classroom, keep in mind the following:

1. Let children translate a pattern made with one type of material into a pattern using another material. For example, when children make necklaces with beads, ask them to show you their designs using buttons or macaroni.
2. Translate the pattern into another language or way of representing the pattern. For example, a pattern consisting of short and long horizontal lines can be translated into a clapping and snapping rhythm or a stepping and jumping pattern. An AB AB pattern can be first shown as blocks and then translated into drumbeats (e.g., loud-soft, loud-soft) or musical sounds (e.g., bell-triangle, bell-triangle).
3. Encourage children to translate patterns from the concrete to the symbolic, by asking them to write or draw the pattern. For example, after making a pattern with house keys, ask the child to rerepresent it by drawing the pattern or symbolizing it with lines or pieces of paper.
4. Have children complete a teacher-made pattern or add to one made by a peer. Ask children to do more than just add the next item; have them make the

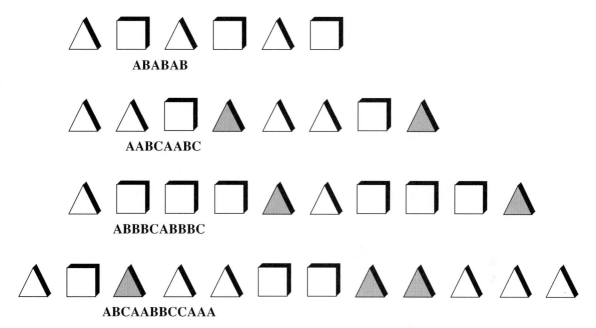

Figure 11.4.   Different types of patterns

entire pattern again. Children should be encouraged to state the pattern verbally. If children cannot do this, the teacher should provide the verbal labels.

5. Encourage children to explain the patterns they create. Sometimes children may not notice that they are making a pattern. For example, children may not realize that laying out the cups and plates for a snack is a pattern.

6. Let several children choose and work on the same pattern. For example, two children might construct a garland of paper links. Let one child put on all the red links while another child puts on all the yellow ones. Children can plan a pattern to work on together or plan one for each other. Let the children decide what pattern they will make. In another example of pairing, one child draws (models) a pattern for another child to reproduce. Children can also translate each other's patterns into another type of material or medium.

7. Use external mediators to help children sort. Use boxes, hoops, or sorting trays labeled with the primary attributes used for sorting. Use words or symbols to label. Figure 11.5 shows the use of sorting hoops; mediation is also provided by the graph being filled out.

Materials.   Some suggestions are pattern blocks, Cuisinaire rods, beads, buttons, seeds, and shells.

Evaluating Learning

1. Can the child complete a pattern, label a known pattern, finish a given pattern, or create his own patterns? Do these patterns become more complex?

Figure 11.5. Children using hoops and a graph for sorting

2. Is there growth in the child's ability to translate patterns from one material, medium, or symbolic system to another? Is the child able to translate only using the same material (e.g., from a pattern of blue and green beads to pattern of red and white beads), or can the child move from one material into another (e.g., from pattern blocks to colored paper)? Can the child translate from one "language" to another (e.g., from a pattern of parquet blocks to drawing or writing)?
3. Is there growth in the child's ability to verbalize and communicate a pattern to another person?

Dramatic Play

Purpose of Activity

Dramatic play is an activity that fosters all higher mental functions, self-regulation, and symbolic functioning (see Chapter 10). Since children perform at the higher level of their ZPD during play, almost any child-generated theme or theme that emerges out of stories or movies can promote development. Children should be encouraged to articulate what they will do in their play before starting, even if the play then takes a dramatic turn and deviates from that starting point. Play should extend for more than just one day, with the activity ending by planning for tomorrow. The next day should begin with a review and possible revision of the last day's play scenario.

Teacher suggestions and guidance are most important when any of the following things happen:

1. Children do not talk to each other.
2. Children exclude a specific child.
3. Few roles emerge.
4. Children do not pretend.
5. Children do not use objects to stand for other objects.
6. Play is fleeting, lasting only 2 or 3 minutes.
7. Only isolated themes emerge, without being integrated into one common theme. Play ends when a new idea is introduced, instead of being adapted to the new idea.

When any of the above things happen, teachers will have to guide play more directly by suggesting how to include other children, proposing a "plot" or roles, asking questions, or even coaching specific children.

Materials.   Use the materials that are usually available in the dramatic play area. The more unspecific the materials the better, so that children use different objects to stand for others, such as a block for a phone, a piece of paper for food, a big box for a spaceship, and a chair for a bus. Have child-size pieces of brightly colored material that children can use to create costumes. Put away the plastic hamburgers!

Evaluating Learning
1. Is there growth in the child's ability to use objects symbolically? Is this use limited only to objects that look like what they represent (e.g., a doll and a baby)? Can the child create a new symbolic substitute when the familiar one is not available?
2. Is there growth in the child's use of language in play? Can the child's partners in play understand how this child uses objects symbolically?
3. Is the child's repertoire of play themes expanding? Is he able to integrate new themes into ongoing play?
4. Is there growth in the number of roles the child plays? Can the child stay in the role for longer and longer periods of time? Can the child play different roles in different plays or within the same play? Is the child able to incorporate new roles into ongoing play?
5. Is there growth in the child's ability to extend play from one day to another? Does the child plan future play with other children?

Storytelling

Purpose of Activity
Storytelling is usually considered beneficial for language development and creativity. In the Vygotskian framework it is also used to promote the development of deliberate memory, logical thinking, and self-regulation. When children retell stories

or create stories, they are not absolutely free in their choice of episodes; the story must make sense to other people. In this way, storytelling is similar to play; both lead children from spontaneous to deliberate behaviors.

By retelling familiar stories and creating their own stories, children learn about general patterns common to all stories. Using these patterns, called *story grammar,* involves putting events in a logical sequence and understanding why a specific sequence is appropriate. Story grammar imposes limits on the content of a story. For example, children learn that if a main character disappears, he will not be able to do anything until something magical takes place to reintroduce the character. By developing the idea of story grammar, children master basic logical concepts such as cause and effect, mutually exclusive events, and so on.

Procedure

Children cannot learn about the logic of a story merely by listening to the teacher read. Listening helps children understand fairly simple texts. More complex stories require much more contextual support, such as external mediators and the children's use of language.

In the beginning, 3- and 4-year-old children will need assistance in retelling simple stories. Provide simple external mediators to help the child remember the sequence of events. These mediators can be teacher-generated at first and then child-generated. It is very important that a child learns to use her own symbols to keep a story line straight. The pictures or scribbles need to make sense only to the child, and can be different from the ones in the book. Make the purpose of the mediator explicit to the child, for example, by saying "These pictures will help you remember the story."

After retelling the story, children can be encouraged to alter the sequence of pictures to see how that might change the story. For example, the teacher can rearrange the pictures for *Goldilocks and the Three Bears* so that Goldilocks is eating the bears' porridge before she goes to the bears' house. Ask the children if the pictures still make sense in this sequence.

Older children can mentally experiment with the elements of a story without much external support. They can be given different versions of the same story to compare, such as the traditional or Disney version of *The Three Little Pigs* and *The Real Story of the Three Little Pigs* by Jon Scieszka. Older children can also practice creating new episodes when given the beginning of a story line, or they can choose various different endings to a story, as in the *Choose Your Own Adventure* series.

To help children make the transition from retelling familiar stories to creating stories of their own, we recommend using the techniques developed by Gianni Rodari, and implemented by teachers in Reggio Emilia, Italy (Edwards, Gandini, & Foreman, 1994). Rodari suggests combining two episodes or characters from different stories (the less compatible they seem, the better) and using this combination as a starting point for a new story. For example, using *Sleeping Beauty,* the teacher could ask children to imagine what might happen if, instead of a prince, the Big Bad Wolf woke up Sleeping Beauty.

Materials.   Books, pictures, puppets will be needed.

Evaluating Learning

1. Is there growth in the child's ability to retell a familiar story? Can the child use the major elements of the story? Do the episodes follow each other logically?
2. Is there growth in the child's ability to remember a story? When the child retells a familiar story, are there missing episodes or episodes that are different from the original? What kind of assistance or external support does the child need to retell a story (e.g., external mediators, prompts from peers, or hints from the teacher)?
3. Is there growth in the child's ability to comprehend stories? What are the elements of the story that the child focuses on when comparing different stories? Are these elements essential for comprehension or just superficial?
4. Can the child change elements of the story and still generate a story line that makes sense?

Journal Writing

Purpose of Activity

Journal writing is a meaningful activity that helps children master written speech, and it is a means for learning specific literacy skills, such as sound-letter correspondence and the function of punctuation. Journal writing and writers' workshop provide a context for writing and opportunities for the child to communicate with others by writing. Thus they become more deliberate in their thinking and their writing. As children write, they must use their literacy skills to create meaningful sentences.

Young children have a hard time making the transition from dictating to the teacher to writing independently. Their dictated stories may be full of imagination and detail, but when asked to write on their own, the stories become simpler, dropping back to a more primitive level. (see Figure 11.6). Some children refuse to write and will only draw. Others write only the first letter of each word even though they show greater awareness of sound-letter correspondence when reading simple books. This transition from total teacher assistance to independence is difficult because children lack the focused attention, deliberate memory, and self-reflective behavior that facilitate their writing. To provide assistance for the writing process, we have developed the scaffolded writing.

Procedure

Scaffolded writing involves using different types of assistance, provided first by the teacher, then by peers, and finally by the child alone. The assistance involves a number of techniques that support the child's deliberate memory and attention. The techniques will vary depending on the kinds of problems the child has as a beginning writer. Many of these techniques help the child to focus on a particular attribute of what she is writing, such as the stem on a letter, the length of a word, or the ending punctuation of a sentence. Once the child notices the attribute, the technique helps the child to reflect on it. This reflection supports memory so that the child can later produce the appropriate attribute. The following suggestions address the most common problems.

Figure 11.6. Child's writing before using the scaffolded writing technique

1. *Remembering how to write a word.* Among the first words that children write usually include their own name and the names of other people or objects. Three- and four-year-old children may attempt to put letters, letter-like symbols, or scribbles on paper to stand for a name. At the beginning they are satisfied with their own writing, but as time goes on, they begin to ask the teacher how to write or spell things, realizing that only certain letters represent a specific name or word. At this point, teachers may write the word, sounding it out with the child, or give the child the word and help the child write out each letter.

When children express an interest in learning to write on their own or when the teacher wants to encourage more independence, the teacher can scaffold the move to independence by writing a line for each letter of the word. The most common use of this technique is helping children learn to write their own names at the top of their work products. The teacher can make a small line for each letter in the name ahead of time or as the child finishes a piece of work, such as a drawing or collage. When the name is particularly long or difficult, the teacher can fill in some of the letters to scaffold the child's writing. A transitional step to complete independence would be having the child make the lines himself and then fill in the letters. For example, a teacher might tell 5-year-old Madeleine that there are nine letters in her first name and help her to write lines for each letter.

2. *Writing sentences.* Use a highlighter to help the child plan the sentence before writing it. When the child dictates, instead of writing down the child's words, make a highlighted line for each word. For example, if the child dictates, "There were three bears at home," you would make six lines that correspond in length to the words the child will write: _____ ____ _____ ____ __ ____. The child should dictate one sentence at a time. Explain that the lines will help the child remember what he is trying to write. Then, point to each line and say the appropriate word with him. Make sure that the child can repeat the words back in the correct order. Then return the sheet to the child and have him write the words on the lines. Figure 11.7 shows a sentence written by the same child that wrote the sample in Figure 11.6 after one week of using the highlighter.

For the first few times through, you will have to model the entire process, writing both the lines and then writing the words on the lines as the child watches. If the lines do not seem to prompt the child's memory when writing, place the first letter(s) of each word on the line, for example:

Th_____ w_____ th_____ b_____ a___ h_____.

Once the child has mastered using the teacher-generated lines, the next step is to use peers to generate the lines for each other. One child says what she wants to write, and the other child makes a line for each word. Children can be paired with a partner at any reading level. Even nonreading children can help readers plan sentences because the reader will speak slowly, pausing between words, which will cue the nonreader that there should be a space and another line. The next step is for the child to generate the line for himself. Some children, especially in first and second grade, resist having a partner make the lines and prefer to generate their own lines after the teacher models.

AMANda.a.J

the cats wr
sit at the
tabl.

Figure 11.7. Child's writing 1 week after using scaffolded writing

3. *Remembering what to write.* Another technique to support memory is to have a *say back buddy.* The say back buddy's job is to help you remember what you want to write. You tell your buddy what you plan to write, and the say back buddy repeats what you have just told her. Children can be paired at different levels. Even nonreaders can help good readers and writers remember long sentences or complicated story plots. At the same time, the nonreader is given practice at deliberate memory which will enhance and improve her reading and writing performance.

4. *Spelling and punctuation.* In first and second grade, children begin to make the transition to conventional spelling and the use of proper grammatical constructions. Many children have trouble applying spelling and grammar rules to their own writing, although they do well on grammar exercises or spelling tests. To support the transfer of these skills, the reflective reading/writing process uses a number of different mediators and types of assistance.

Put the rule or the set of spelling words on a card the child will use as an external mediator during writing. After the child has written a sentence, have him look at the mediator card and compare it to his own writing. The child should then highlight the punctuation mark or the spelling word that matches the one on the card and check to see whether his writing "looks right." If there is a misspelled word, the child should correct it. After self-checking, the child should work with a buddy, who will check to make sure that the child has used the mediator card correctly and has highlighted the right things. Only after checking with a buddy does the teacher see the work.

Some children have trouble moving from the role of writer to editor. The flow of writing is disrupted because they refuse to write without editing (correcting all their mistakes). Others never edit. To help children keep these roles distinct use specific external mediators for each. Use a special pen for writing—and only for writing. Have a pair of "editor's eyes" (eyeglass frames or a magnifying glass) and a special editor's pen of a different color than the writer's pen.

Materials.   Highlighters, colored pens and pencils, mediator cards, letter strips, writing rings, and stickers are useful.

Evaluating Learning

1. Does the mediator prompt appropriate behavior? For example, does the mediator remind the child to remember how to write sentences?

2. Can the child use the mediator without direct teacher support?

3. Can the child express the reason for using the mediator? Can the child explain the reasons to another child?

4. Does the problem the child had gradually decrease or disappear?

Reading

Purpose of Activity

Certain underlying cognitive skills pose problems for some children as they acquire reading skills. The scaffolded reading technique provides support for these underlying skills, allowing children to take more mental actions while reading and consequently appropriate skills more easily.

Procedure

The procedures used depend on the type of problem that the child has.

1. *Following along during group reading.* During oral reading many teachers have children follow along in their books with their fingers or with a bookmark. This is not very effective because some children run their fingers across the page or move the bookmark in an automatic, thoughtless manner. When teachers have children use highlighters on laminated books, highlighting each word as they read, children seem to become more engaged. Using laminated books or covering the page with acetate film (overhead projector sheets), have the child highlight the words as they are read. If the child highlights entire lines, explain that she is to highlight only the words that are read, as they are read.

2. *Reading certain parts of a word.* Typical mistakes are reading only the first letters and skipping internal vowels or the latter part of the word. Once you are sure that a certain pattern of mistakes is typical for a particular child, you can use a highlighter to support the child's reading of the missing portion of the word. Using laminated books or acetate film laid over regular book pages, have the child go over the page prior to reading and highlight the end of each word or the internal vowels. This step can be combined with the use of a mediator card to prompt memory of specific vowels or consonant-vowel combinations. While highlighting, have the child use private speech to say what she is highlighting and why. For example, a child highlighting *ing* might say, "ing—remember to read *ing.*" After highlighting, the child reads the passage.

3. *Reading certain words.* For some children, the problem is confusing words that look similar to each other, such as *saw* and *was, said* and *and, it* and *is, where* and *when.* This type of repeated error can be corrected by using a highlighter also. In this case, have the child highlight one word in one color and the other word in another color prior to reading the passage. As the child highlights, encourage private speech that helps the child keep the words straight. The child might say, "This is *was* so I make it green" and "this is *saw* so I make it red."

4. *Using reading strategies.* A child may know and be able to describe a reading strategy when asked but not able to apply the strategy when actually reading text. To promote the use of strategies while reading, place the written-out strategy on a card that the child can refer to while reading. For example, the card might read, "When I don't know a word, I skip it and come back to it later" or "Look at the word to see if it is like another word I know." Have the child highlight the words he is not sure of. Then have the child read the strategies as he looks at the highlighted word and identify which one works. This can be done individually or with a buddy.

Materials.   Highlighters, acetate film, and laminated books are needed.

Evaluating Learning

1. Can the child use the mediator appropriately and eventually correctly?
2. Can the child voice the reasons for using the highlighter? Can the child explain to a peer how and why the highlighter is used?
3. Can the child transfer the use of the mediator from one reading setting to another? Can the child use the highlighter in small-group reading and then in large-group or silent reading?
4. Does the child progress in skill acquisition? Do specific problems persist or get better?

Large-Muscle Activities

Purpose of the Activity

To help children develop better large muscle control, which will lead to better cognitive and emotional self-regulation, teachers in Vygotskian-based classrooms use several types of large-muscle activities. By practicing deliberate motor control, children learn to master their own cognitive behavior. Consequently, all of these exercises and games involve the inhibition of reactive movements until the correct verbal command is given.

Procedure

Games such as Simon Says, Freeze, Follow the Leader, and Duck, Duck, Goose all require that the child wait until there is a verbal command before moving. The commands can be given by other children or by the teacher. Songs in which children must make a specific movement along with the words, finger plays, and acting out stories also require the inhibition of motor behavior.

Activities such as hopscotch, jump rope, clapping to a beat, and hopping to a beat all require specific motor responses. These are more difficult than games like Simon Says because the child must hop only at a certain place or clap in a specific way.

Games with specific rules are also excellent for promoting motor control in older children. These games can be simple, such as Red Rover, or they can be complex, as in soccer or baseball.

Modify games in which children take turns by passing around an external mediator such as a ball or stick as a signal for "my turn to talk." Teachers have used this technique during circle time to help children take turns talking. One teacher has a welcome song in which all of the children say their names. She uses a beanbag man who is passed from child to child as each says his or her name.

Evaluating Learning

1. Can the child inhibit his or her behavior and play the game? How much teacher support is needed (e.g., repeating the rules, giving hints). Can children play the game unassisted?

2. What kind of behavior seems to be the easiest for the child to control and the hardest to control? For some children, stopping a movement is more difficult than starting it.

Small-Muscle Activities

Purpose of the Activity

Small motor control refers to use of the hands and hand-eye coordination. Early childhood activities that promote small-muscle development include using modeling clay, art activities, writing and drawing, pasting and gluing, beading, and cutting with a scissors. These activities can help children become more deliberate in their small-muscle actions and master various materials. For example, they learn to plan how they will cut out objects instead of just cutting and snipping chaotically. Developmentally, small-muscle control is one of the last to develop, but it is common knowledge that children who have not mastered some small-muscle tasks have problems in first and second grade.

The emphasis in the Vygotskian approach is on learning to use the instrument or material appropriately and efficiently, not on the precision of the final product. By using tools and materials to make things, children develop strategies that they can apply to other learning.

Procedure

1. *Holding an instrument correctly*. Sometimes children hold the pencil, paintbrush, or scissors in such a way that it impedes their ability to use the instrument. Teachers may have to model how to hold the instrument because children, although they may have seen adults holding it correctly, often do not focus on the most important attributes of the grip. Describe what you do with your hands in words so that the child can use private speech to guide him. For example, say, "To move the scissors, squeeze, squeeze."

Some children may need external mediators to remind them of the correct position of the fingers on the instrument. For example, you can put a dot on one side of the paper to remind children to hold the paper being cut with the dot under their thumb. Tell them to cut "with thumbs up."

To form letters properly a child must hold the pencil in a three-point grasp. We suggest using a variety of mediators to remind the child of the proper grip paired with language that makes your expectations clear to the child. To introduce the proper grip, place a sticker in the hollow between the thumb and index finger while you explain that the sticker will help the child remember where the end of the pencil should point. Use pencils with plastic grips or triangular pencils that promote the three-point grasp. Once children become accustomed to holding the pencil correctly, you can graduate to a "writing ring" which is worn only when writing. Be sure to encourage the use of private speech. The child should say, "The sticker reminds me where the pencil goes" or "The writing ring reminds me to hold my pencil correctly."

2. *Forming letters.* First- and second-grade teachers use many different techniques to support forming letters from giving penmanship instruction to supplying letter strips and dotted letters that the child traces with a finger or pencil. It is important that children use private speech to make explicit their actions and the purpose of the mediator. In addition, the mediators used should not only be salient but close to the child physically. Thus, having letter strips that the child gets out only for writing and puts on her desk at that time is better than having letter strips taped to the desk or placed on the chalkboard.

If the child is having trouble forming specific letters, such as reversing *b* and *d,* then additional support will be necessary. Place the letters that are confusing on a card that the child will have in front of her as she writes. Write the troublesome letters in colors that are different from the pen or pencil used to write all other letters. For example, make the *b* blue and the *d* green. Have the child write all letters in regular pencil. When the child comes to a *b* or a *d,* have her check the mediator card and decide whether to write the letter in blue or green. For example, the child should say to herself, "It is a *b,* so it goes this way and is blue," as she writes the letter in blue, and vice versa for the letter *d.* As the child is able to perform the task correctly, remove the mediator card. Later, remove the colored pencils.

Materials.   Stickers, rings, pencil grips, and colored pencils are needed.

Evaluating Learning

1. Can the child use the instrument appropriately? How independent is the child from teacher reminders? Remember that 3 and 4 year olds may not be able to perform with precision or consistency and that this is developmentally appropriate.

2. Can the child follow directions for the activity? How many mediators are needed to help the child perform at the highest level of her ZPD?

Epilogue

In our work with teachers over the past three years, many have remarked to us that studying Vygotsky has been rejuvenating and exciting because it confirms for them so many of the things that they know work in their classrooms. His ideas fill in the reasons for their practice, providing the explanation for their intuitive actions. In addition Vygotsky gives them a new way of looking at their role, a way to analyze what they need to do without denying the fact that children are active participants in learning. Instead of only having the option of following the child's lead or acting as the taskmaster, teachers now have more ways of assisting performance.

Another strength of the Vygotskian approach is its emphasis on the underlying cognitive skills that parents and teachers are concerned about: self-regulation, deliberate memory, and focused attention. Many teachers have noted how changing these skills can have a radical effect on a child's entire outlook on school. Many of the children who have gained in self-regulation in academic tasks show improved social skills and a more positive attitude toward school.

Finally, and most exciting, the Vygotskian-based activities we have tried are extremely effective in the classroom. Interventions that we have designed using this model have had a positive impact on learning and classroom interactions. This has been the most heartening result of all!

The year 1996 marks the 100th anniversary of the birth of both Vygotsky and Piaget (these two giants of developmental psychology were born only three months apart). While there has been much research and many classroom applications of Piaget's work, up until quite recently there has been little application of Vygotsky's ideas in the early childhood classroom. We hope that this anniversary will be marked by a renewed interest in Vygotsky's research and the application of his ideas to the early childhood classroom.

Glossary

This glossary contains words that are referred to frequently in the text and that have different meanings in the Vygotskian framework than in general usage.

Amplification

A technique for assisting behaviors on the edge of emergence using the tools and assisted performance within the child's ZPD; the opposite of acceleration, or pushing the child too fast.

Appropriation of knowledge

The stage when the child has internalized or learned certain information or concepts and can use that knowledge independently.

Complex

A set of undifferentiated attributes used to categorize objects. For example, a child might use the complex "big-round-red" to understand "ball." Complexes exist before the development of concepts.

Cultural-Historical Theory

The name given to the Vygotskian approach which emphasizes the cultural context of learning and development and the history of the human mind.

Deliberate memory

When children can remember on purpose, using memory strategies and mediators, they have deliberate memory. They no longer require many reminders from the environment but make the mental effort necessary to remember.

Developmental accomplishments

The new cognitive and emotional formations that appear at different ages.

Director's play

Play in which children play with pretend playmates or direct and act out a scene with toys without anyone else present.

Distributed
>   Shared or existing between two or more people.

Double stimulation (microgenetic method)
>   A research method in which the child is taught something new through the use of mental tools (e.g., symbols, categories). The researcher notes both what the child is able to learn and how the tools are being learned.

Dynamic assessment
>   A classroom assessment technique that measures both the upper and lower levels of the ZPD.

Educational dialogue
>   The exchange that occurs when the teacher sensitively guides the discussion and the child explains her understanding of the information; similar to the Socratic dialogue.

Emotional communication
>   The emotional dialogue between the infant and the primary caregiver; the developmental accomplishment of infancy.

Everyday concepts
>   Concepts based on intuitions and everyday experience. They do not have strict definitions nor are they integrated into a broader structure.

Focused attention
>   The ability to attend deliberately and to ignore distractions.

Games
>   A type of play in which the rules are explicit and roles are implicit; most typical of children age 6 and 7.

Higher mental functions
>   Cognitive processes unique to humans and acquired through learning and teaching. They are deliberate, mediated, internalized behaviors built upon lower mental functions. Examples are mediated perception, focused attention, deliberate memory, self-regulation, and other metacognitive processes.

Inner speech
>   Speech that is totally internal, inaudible, self-directed, but retains some of the characteristics of external speech. People use inner speech talk to themselves, hearing the words but not saying them aloud.

Internalization
>   The process of appropriation or learning to the point at which the tools used are mental and their use is not visible to others.

Interpersonal (interindividual, shared)
>   Describing the stage of using mental tools with others or sharing the mental tools with others.

Intrapersonal (individual)
>   Describing the stage when mental tools have been internalized and are used independently.

Leading activity
>   A specific type of interaction between the child and the social environment that is most beneficial for the emergence of developmental accomplishments.

Learning activity
> Adult-guided activity around specific, structured, formalized content that is culturally determined; the leading activity of the primary grades. Learning activity is found in schools where children begin to acquire basic literacies, such as concepts in math, science, and history; images in art and literature; and the rules of grammar.

Level of assisted performance
> Behaviors that the child can perform with the help of or through interacting with another person, either an adult or peer. Assistance can be direct or indirect, such as choosing a book or materials.

Level of independent performance
> Behaviors that the child can perform alone and without help; the lowest level of the ZPD.

Lower mental functions
> Cognitive processes common to both higher animals and human beings which depend primarily on maturation to develop. Examples are sensations, reactive attention, spontaneous memory, and sensorimotor intelligence.

Maximally assisted performance
> Behaviors the child can perform with the most help or assistance from the social context; the highest level of the ZPD. These behaviors will become what the child can do independently at a later time.

Mediation
> The use of an object or symbol to represent a specific behavior or another object in the environment. For example, the word *red* mediates the perception of colors.

Mediator
> Something that stands as an intermediary between the child and the environment and that facilitates a particular behavior. A mediator becomes a mental tool when the child incorporates it into her own activity. Examples are a string around a finger, a list, a rhyme, and a clock face.

Mental Tools
> Internalized tools that extend mental abilities, helping us to remember, attend, and solve problems. Mental tools are different in each culture and are taught to succeeding generations. They help the child master his own behavior. Examples are language and mediators.

Nonpragmatic curiosity
> Interest that exists although there may be no tangible or practical payoff; similar to intrinsic motivation.

Other-regulation
> The state in which the child regulates other people or is regulated by other people; the opposite of self-regulation.

Play
> Interaction that involves explicit roles and implicit rules; the leading activity for the preschool-age child.

Private speech
> Self-directed speech that is not intended for communication to others. Private speech is turned inward to self and has a self-regulatory function.

Public speech

Language directed at others that has a social, communicative function. Public speech is spoken aloud and directs or communicates to others.

Repeated errors

Errors that are not developmental or part of the learning process. These types of errors are often recognized by the learner as mistakes, but the learner cannot seem to stop repeating them. Repeated errors tend to persist in spite of efforts to correct them. They are often the result of having automatized an action incorrectly.

Scaffolding

The process of providing, and gradually removing, external support for learning. During scaffolding, the task itself is not changed, but what the learner initially does is made easier with assistance. As the learner takes more responsibility for performance of the task, less assistance is provided.

Scientific concepts

Concepts taught within a discipline that has its own logical structure and vocabulary.

Self-regulation

The state in which the child is able to regulate or master his own behavior; the opposite of other-regulation. The child can plan, monitor, evaluate, and choose his own behavior.

Shared

Existing between two or more people.

Social Context

Everything in the child's environment that has either been directly or indirectly influenced by the culture. This includes people (e.g., parents, teachers, peers) and materials (e.g., books, videos).

Socially mediated

Influenced by present and past social interactions. Interaction with the environment is always mediated by others.

Socially shared cognition

Mental processes, such as memory and attention, that are shared or exist between two or more people.

Social situation of development

The social context and the way the child reacts to this context.

Symbolic function

The use of objects, actions, words, and people to stand for something else. Examples are using a pencil as a spaceship or a book as a bed for a doll.

Verbal thinking

A type of thinking that is more distilled than inner speech and is what Vygotsky called "folded." When thinking is folded, you can think of several things simultaneously and may not be conscious of all that you are thinking.

Zone of Proximal Development (ZPD)

Those behaviors that are on the edge of emergence. It is defined by two levels. The lowest level is what the child can do independently and the highest level is what the child can do with maximum assistance.

References

The names of the Russian authors in this reference list have been romanized in a number of different ways. We have used the most common spelling; alternative spellings are provided below.

Common	Alternative
Vygotsky	Vygotski, Vigotsky, Vygotskij
Luria	Lurija, Lur'ia
Elkonin	El'konin
Gal'perin	Galperin
Leont'ev	Leontjev

Atkinson, R. C., & Shiffrin, R. M. (1968). Human Memory: A proposed system and its control processes. In K. W. Spence & J. T. Spence (Eds.), *Advances in the psychology of learning and motivation* (Vol. 2, pp. 90–195). New York: Academic Press.

Azmitia, M. (1992). Expertise, private speech, and the development of self-regulation. In R. M. Diaz & L. E. Berk (Eds.), *Private speech: From social interaction to self-regulation* (pp. 101–122). Hillsdale, NJ: Lawrence Erlbaum.

Beilin, H. (1994). Jean Piaget's enduring contribution to developmental psychology. In R. D. Parke, P. A. Ornstein, J. J. Reiser, & C. Zahn-Waxler (Eds.), *A century of developmental psychology* (pp. 333–356). Washington, DC : American Psychological Association.

Berk, L. E. (1992). Children's private speech: An overview of theory and the status of research. In R. M. Diaz & L. E. Berk (Eds.), *Private speech: From social interaction to self-regulation* (pp. 17–53). Hillsdale, NJ: Lawrence Erlbaum.

Berk, L. E. (1994). *Child Development* (3rd ed.). Boston: Allyn & Bacon.

Berk, L. E. (1994). Vygotsky's theory: The importance of make believe play. *Young Children, 50* (1), 30-39.

Berk, L. E. & Winsler, A. (1995). Scaffolding children's learning: Vygotsky and early childhood education. *NAEYC Research and Practice Series, 7.* Washington, DC: National Assocation for the Education of Young Children.

Bivens, J. A., & Berk, L. E. (1990). Longitudinal study of the development of elementary school children's private speech. *Merrill-Palmer Quarterly, 36,* 443–463.

Bodrova, E., & Leong, D. J. (1995). Scaffolding the writing process: The Vygotskian approach. *Colorado Reading Council Journal, 6,* 27–29.

Bowlby, J. (1969). *Attachment and loss: Vol. 1. Attachment.* New York: Basic Books.

Bredecamp, S. (Ed.). (1992). *Developmentally appropriate practice in early childhood programs serving children from birth to age 8* (Rev. ed.). Washington, DC: National Association for the Education of Young Children.

Bretherton, I. (1992). The origins of attachment theory: John Bowlby and Mary Ainsworth. *Developmental Psychology, 28,* 759–775.

Bretherton, I., & Walters, E. (Eds.). (1985). Growing points of attachment. *Monographs of the Society for Research in Child Development, 50* (1–2, serial no. 209).

Brofman, V. V. (1991). *Means of mediating constructive activity in preschool children.* Paper presented at the colloquium sponsored by the Department of Curriculum & Instruction, University of Wisconsin-Madison.

Bronckart, J-P., & Ventouras-Spycher, M. (1979). The Piagetian concept of representation and the Soviet-inspired view of self-regulation. In G. Ziven (Ed.), *The development of self-regulation through private speech* (pp. 99–131). New York: John Wiley & Sons.

Bronfenbrenner, U. (1977). Toward an experimental ecology of human development. *American Psychologist, 32,* 513–531.

Brown, A. L. (1978). Knowing when, where, and how to remember: A problem of metacognition. In R. Glaser (Ed.), *Advances in instructional psychology* (Vol. 1, pp. 77–165). Hillsdale, NJ: Erlbaum.

Brown, A. L., Ash, D., Rutherford, M., Nakagawa, K., Gordon, A., & Campione, J. C. (1993). Distributed expertise in the classroom. In G. Salomon (Ed.), *Distributed cognition: Psychological and educational considerations* (pp. 188–208). Cambridge: Cambridge University Press.

Brown, A. L., & Ferrara, R. A. (1985). Diagnosing the zones of proximal development. In J. Wertsch (Ed.), *Culture, communication and cognition: Vygotskian perspectives* (pp. 273–305). Cambridge: Cambridge University Press.

Brownell, C. A., & Carriger, M. S. (1991). Collaborations among toddler peers: Individual contributions to social contexts. In L. B. Resnick, J. M. Levine, & S. D. Teasley (Eds.), *Perspectives on socially shared cognition* (pp. 365–383). Washington, DC: American Psychological Association.

Bruner, J. S. (1968). *Process of cognitive growth: Infancy.* Worcester, MA: Clark University Press.

Bruner, J. S. (1983). Vygotsky's zone of proximal development: The hidden agenda. *New Directions for Child Development, 23,* 93–97.

Bruner, J. S. (1985). Vygotsky: A historical and conceptual perspective. In J. Wertsch (Ed.), *Culture, communication and cognition: Vygotskian perspectives* (pp. 21–34). Cambridge: Cambridge University Press.

Campione, J. C., & Brown, A. L. (1990). Guided learning and transfer. In N. Fredriksen, R. Glaser, A. Lesgold, & M. Shafto (Eds.), *Diagnostic monitoring of skill and knowledge acquisition* (pp. 141–172). Hillsdale, NJ: Erlbaum.

Campione, J. C., Brown, A. L., Ferrara, R. A., & Bryant, N. R. (1984). The zone of proximal development: Implications for individual differences and learning. *New Directions for Child Development, 23,* 77–91.

Cannella, G. S. (1993). Learning through social interaction: Shared cognitive experience, negotiation strategies, and joint concept construction for young children. *Early Childhood Research Quarterly, 8,* 427–444.

Cazden, C. B. (1981). Performance before competence: Assistance to child discourse in the zone of proximal development. *Quarterly Newsletter of the Laboratory of Comparative Human Cognition, 3,* 5–8.

Cazden, C. B. (1993). Vygotsky, Hymes, and Bakhtin: From word to utterance to voice. In E. A. Forman, N. Minick, & C. A. Stone (Eds.), *Contexts for learning: Sociocultural dynamics in children's development* (pp. 197–212). New York: Oxford University Press.

Ceci, S. J. (1991). How much does schooling influence general intelligence and its cognitive components? A reassessment of the evidence. *Developmental Psychology, 27*(5), 703–722.

Chang-Wells, G. L. M., & Wells, G. (1993). Dynamics of discourse: Literacy and the construction of knowledge. In E. A. Forman, N. Minick, & C. A. Stone (Eds.), *Contexts for learning: Sociocultural dynamics in children's development* (pp. 58–91). New York: Oxford University Press.

Clay, M. M. (1991). *Becoming literate: The construction of inner control.* Portsmouth, NH: Heineman.

Clay, M. M., & Cazden, C. (1990). A Vygotskian interpretation of reading recovery. In L. Moll (Ed.), *Vygotsky and education: Instructional implications and applications of sociohistorical psychology* (pp. 206–222). Cambridge: Cambridge University Press.

Cobb, P., Wood, T., & Yackel, E. (1993). Discourse, mathematical thinking, and classroom practice. In E. A. Forman, N. Minick, & C. A. Stone (Eds.), *Contexts for learning: Sociocultural dynamics in children's development* (pp. 91–119). New York: Oxford University Press.

Cohen, P., Kulik, J. A., & Kulik, C. C. (1982). Educational outcomes of tutoring. *American Educational Research Journal, 19,* 237–248.

Cole, M. (1977). *Soviet developmental psychology: An anthology.* White Plains, New York: M. E. Sharpe.

Cole, M. (Ed.). (1978). *The selected writings of A. R. Luria.* White Plains, NY: M. E. Sharpe.

Cole, M. (1985). The zone of proximal development: Where culture and cognition create each other. In J. Wertsch (Ed.), *Culture, communication and cognition: Vygotskian perspectives* (pp. 146–182). Cambridge: Cambridge University Press.

Cole, M. (1990). Cognitive development and formal schooling: The evidence from cross-cultural research. In L. Moll (Ed.), *Vygotsky and education: Instructional implications and applications of sociohistorical psychology* (pp. 89–110). Cambridge: Cambridge University Press.

Cole, M. (1994, June). *Cultural mechanisms of cultural development.* Paper presented at the meeting of the Jean Piaget Society, Chicago, IL.

Cole, M., & Engstron, Y. (1993). A cultural historical approach to distributed cognition. In G. Salomon (Ed.), *Distributed cognition: Psychological and educational considerations.* Cambridge: Cambridge University Press.

Cole, M., & Maltzman, I. (Ed.). (1969). *A handbook of contemporary Soviet psychology.* New York: Basic Books.

Cole, M., & Scribner, S. (1973). Cognitive consequences of formal and informal education. *Science, 182,* 553–559.

Cooper, C. R., Marquis, A., & Edward, D. (1986). Four perspectives on peer learning among elementary school children. In E. C. Meuller & C. R. Cooper (Eds.), *Process and outcome in peer relationships* (pp. 3–24). Orlando, FL: Academic Press.

Crain, W. C. (1991). *Theories of development: Concepts and applications.* Englewood Cliffs, NJ: Prentice-Hall.

Cronbach, L. J. (1990). *Essentials of psychological testing* (5th ed.). New York: Harper & Row.

D'Ailly, Hsiao, H. (1992). Asian mathematics superiority: A search for explanations. *Educational Psychologist, 27*(2), 243–261.

Damon, W. (1991). Problems of direction in socially shared cognition. In L. B. Resnick, J. M. Levine, & S. D. Teasley (Eds.), *Perspectives on socially shared cognition* (pp. 284–397). Washington, DC: American Psychological Association.

Daniels, H. (Ed.). (1993). *Charting the agenda: Education activity after Vygotsky.* London: Routledge.

Davydov, V. V. (1986). *Problemy razvivayuschego obuchenija* [Problems of developing instruction]. Moscow: Pedagogika.

Davydov, V. V. (1988). Problems of developmental teaching: The experience of theoretical and experimental psychological research. *Soviet Education, 30,* 66–79. (Original work published in 1986).

Davydov, V. V. (Ed.). (1991). *Psychological abilities of primary school children in learning mathematics: Vol. 6. Soviet studies in mathematics education* (J. Teller, Trans.). Reston, VA: National Council of Teachers of Mathematics. (Original work published in 1969).

Davydov, V. V., & Markova, A. K. (1983). A concept of educational activity for school children. *Journal of Soviet Psychology, 21*(2), 50–76. (Original work published in 1981).

Davydov, V. V., & Radzikhovskii, L. A. (1985). Vygotsky's theory and the activity-oriented approach in psychology. In J. Wertsch (Ed.), *Culture, communication and cognition: Vygotskian perspectives* (pp. 35–65). Cambridge: Cambridge University Press.

Davydov, V. V., & Zinchenko, V. P. (1993). Vygotsky's contribution to the development of psychology. In H. Daniels (Ed.), *Charting the agenda: Education activity after Vygotsky.* London: Routledge.

Diaz, R. M., & Berk, L. E. (Eds.). (1992). *Private speech: From social interaction to self-regulation.* Hillsdale, NJ: Lawrence Erlbaum.

Diaz, R. M., Neal, C. J., & Amaya-Williams, M. (1990). The social origins of self-regulation. In L. Moll (Ed.), *Vygotsky and education: Instructional implications and applications of sociohistorical psychology* (127–154). Cambridge: Cambridge University Press.

Edwards, C., Gandini, L., & Forman, G. (1994). *Hundred languages of children: The Reggio Emillia approach to early childhood education.* Chicago: Teachers College Press.

Elkonin, D. (1996). Symbolics and its function in the play of children. *Soviet Education, 8*(2), 35–41.

Elkonin, D. (1969). Some results of the study of the psychological development of preschool-age children. In M. Cole & I. Maltzman (Eds.), *A handbook of contemporary Soviet psychology.* New York: Basic Books.

Elkonin, D. (1977). Toward the problem of stages in the mental development of the child. In M. Cole (Ed.), *Soviet developmental psychology.* White Plains, NY: M. E. Sharpe. (Original work published in 1971).

Elkonin, D. (1978). Psikhologija igry [The psychology of play.] Moscow: Pedagogika.

Erikson, E. E. (1963). *Childhood and society* (2nd ed.). New York: Norton.

Erikson, E. E. (1977). *Toys and reasons.* New York: Norton.

Evans, P. (1993). Some implications of Vygotsky's work for special education. In H. Daniels (Ed.), *Charting the agenda: Education activity after Vygotsky.* London: Routledge.

Feuerstein, R., & Feuerstein, S. (1991). Mediated learning experience: A theoretical review. In R. Feuerstein, P. S. Klein, & A. J. Tannenbaum (Eds.), *Mediated learning experience (MLE): Theoretical, psychological and learning implications.* London, Freund.

Feuerstein, R., Haywood, H. K., Rand, Y., Hoffman, M. B., & Jensen, M. R. (1986). *Learning potential assessment device.* Jerusalem: Hadassah/Canada Research Institute.

Flavell, J. H. (1994). Cognitive development: Past, present and future. In R. D. Parke, P. A. Ornstein, J. J. Reiser, & C. Zahn-Waxler (Eds.), *A century of developmental psychology.* Washington, DC: American Psychological Association.

Forman, E. A., & Cazden, C. (1985). Exploring Vygotskian perspectives in education: The cognitive value of peer interaction. In J. Wertsch (Ed.), *Culture, communication and cognition: Vygotskian perspectives* (pp. 323–349). Cambridge: Cambridge University Press.

Forman, E. A., & McPhail, J. (1993). Vygotskian perspectives on children's collaborative problem-solving activities. In E. A. Forman, N. Minick, & C. A. Stone (Eds.), *Contexts for learning: Sociocultural dynamics in children's development* (pp. 19–42). New York: Oxford University Press.

Frankel, K., & Bates, J. (1990). Mother-toddler problem solving: Antecedents in attachment, home behavior, and temperament. *Child Development, 61,* 810–819.

Frauenglass, M. H., & Diaz, R. M. (1985). Self-regulatory functions of children's private speech: A critical analysis of recent challenges to Vygotsky's theory. *Developmental Psychology, 21,* 357–364.

Freud, A. (1966). Introduction to the technique of child analysis. In *The writings of Anna Freud* (Vol. 1, p. 3069). New York: International Universities Press. (Original work published as *Four lectures on child analysis,* 1927).

Freud, S. (1961). *Beyond the pleasure principle.* New York: Norton.

Gage, N. L., & Berliner, D. C. (1992). *Educational psychology* (5th ed.). Boston: Houghton Mifflin.

Gallimore, R., & Tharp, R. (1990). Teaching mind in society: Teaching, schooling, and literate discourse. In L. Moll (Ed.), *Vygotsky and education: Instructional implications and applications of sociohistorical psychology* (pp. 175–205). Cambridge: Cambridge University Press.

Gal'perin, P. Y. (1969). Stages of development of mental acts. In M. Cole & I. Maltzman (Eds.), *A handbook of contemporary soviet psychology* (pp. 249–273). New York: Basic Books.

Gal'perin, P. Y. (1979). The role of orientation in thought. *Soviet Psychology, 18*(2), 84–99. (Original work published in 1972).

Gal'perin, P. Y. (1992a). Organization of mental activity and the effectiveness of learning. *Journal of Russian and East European Psychology, 30*(4), 65–82. (Original work published in 1974).

Gal'perin, P. Y. (1992b). The problem of attention. *Journal of Russian and East European Psychology, 30*(4), 83–91. (Original work published in 1976).

Garvey, C. (1986). Peer relations and the growth of communication. In E. C. Mueller & C. R. Cooper (Eds.), *Process and outcome in peer relationships* (pp. 329–344). San Diego, CA: Academic Press.

Gellatly, A. R. H. (1987). Acquisition of a concept of logical necessity. *Human Development, 30,* 32–47.

Ginsberg, H. P., & Opper, S. (1988). *Piaget's theory of intellectual development* (3rd ed.). Englewood Cliffs, NJ: Prentice Hall.

Godovikova, D. B. (1991). Forms of communication with an adult as a factor in the development of the preschool child's cognitive activity. *Soviet Psychology, 29*(1), 62–72.

Goodman, Y. M., & Goodman, K. S. (1990). Vygotsky in a whole-language perspective. In L. Moll (Ed.), *Vygotsky and education: Instructional implications and applications of sociohistorical psychology* (pp. 223–250). Cambridge: Cambridge University Press.

Grossman K. E., & Grossman, K. (1990). The wider concept of attachment in cross-cultural research. *Human Development, 13,* 31–47.

Haywood, H. C., & Tzuriel, D. (Eds.). (1992). *Interactive assessment.* New York: Springer-Verlag.

Hedegaard, M. (1990). The zone of proximal development as the basis for instruction. In L. Moll (Ed.), *Vygotsky and education: Instructional implications and applications of sociohistorical psychology* (pp. 349–372). Cambridge: Cambridge University Press.

Hickman, M. E. (1985). The implications of discourse skills in Vygotsky's developmental theory. In J. Wertsch (Ed.), *Culture, communication and cognition: Vygotskian perspectives* (pp. 236–258). Cambridge: Cambridge University Press.

Horowitz, F. D. (1994). John B. Watson's legacy: Learning and environment. In R. D. Parke, P. A. Ornstein, J. J. Rieser, & C. Zahn-Waxler (Eds.), *A century of developmental psychology.* (pp. 233–250). Washington, DC: American Psychological Association.

Howes, C. (1980). Peer play scale as an index of complexity of peer interaction. *Developmental Psychology, 16,* 371–379.

Howes, C., & Matheson, C. C. (1992). Sequences in the development of competent play with peers: Social and social pretend play. *Developmental Psychology, 28,* 961–974.

Hutt, S. J., Tyler, S., Hutt, C., & Christopherson, H. (1989). *Play, exploration, and learning: A natural history of the pre-school.* London: Routledge.

Hyden, L-C. (1988). *The conceptual structure of Soviet psychology in Vygotskij's, Leontjev's, and Rubinstejn's theories.* Stockholm: University of Stockholm, Department of Psychology.

Inhelder, B., & Piaget, J. S. (1958). *The growth of logical thinking from childhood to adolescence.* (A. Parsons & S. Seagrin, Trans.). New York: Basic Books. (Original work published in 1955).

Istomina, Z. M. (1977). The development of voluntary memory in preschool-age children. In M. Cole (Ed.), *Soviet developmental psychology.* White plains, NY: M. E. Sharpe. (Original work published in 1948).

Jahoda, G. (1980). Theoretical and systematic approaches in mass-cultural psychology. In H. C. Triandis & W. W. Lambert (Eds.), *Handbook of cross-cultural psychology* (Vol. 1). Boston: Allyn and Bacon.

Johnson, D., & Johnson, R. (1991). *Learning together and alone: Cooperation, competition, and individualization* (4th ed.). Boston: Allyn & Bacon.

Johnson, J. E., Christie, J. F., & Yawkey, T. D. (1987). *Play and early childhood development.* Glenview, IL: Scott, Foresman.

John-Steiner, V. (1992). Private speech among adults. In R. M. Diaz & L. E. Berk (Eds.), *Private Speech: From social interaction to self-regulation* (pp. 285–296).

John-Steiner, V., Panofsky, C. P., & Smith, L. W. (Eds.). (1994). *Sociocultural approaches to language and literacy: An interactionist perspective.* Cambridge: Cambridge University Press.

Joravsky, D. (1989). *Russian psychology: A critical history.* Cambridge, MA: Blackwell.

Karpov, Y. V. & Bransford, J. D. (1995). L. S. Vygotsky and the doctrine of empirical and theoretical reasoning. *Educational Psychologist, 30* (2), 61-66.

Katz, L. G., & Chard, S. C. (1989). *Engaging children's minds: The project approach.* Norwood, NJ: Ablex.

Kilpatrick, J. (Ed.) (1972). *Instruction in problem solving.* Chicago: University of Chicago.

Kilpatrick, J. (Ed.). (1975). *The problem of instruction.* Chicago: University of Chicago.

Kohlberg, L. E., Yaeger, J., & Hjertholm, E. (1968). Private speech: Four studies and a review of theories. *Child Development, 39,* 691–736.

Kotyzko, V. K., & Dutkenvich, T. V. (1992). The role of joint activity in the development of cognitive activities in preschoolers. *Journal of Russian and East European Psychology, 30*(3), 57–73.

Kozulin, A. (1984). *Psychology in Utopia: Toward a social history of Soviet psychology.* Cambridge, MA: MIT Press.

Kozulin, A. (1990). *Vygotsky's psychology: A bibliography of ideas.* Cambridge, MA: Harvard University Press.

Kozulin, A., & Presseisen, B. Z. (1995). Mediated learning experience and psychological tools: Vygotsky's and Feuerstein's perspectives in a study of student learning. *Educational Psychologist, 30* (2), 67-76.

Laboratory of Comparative Human Cognition. (1983). Culture and cognitive development. In P. Mussen (Ed.), *Handbook of child psychology: Vol. 1. History, theory, and methods.* New York: Wiley.

Lave, J. (1991). Situated learning in communities of practice. In L. B. Resnick, J. M. Levine, & S. D. Teasley (Eds.), *Perspectives on socially shared cognition.* (pp. 63–84) Washington, DC: American Psychological Association.

Leont'ev, A. (1978). *Activity, consciousness, and personality.* Englewood Cliffs, NJ: Prentice-Hall. (Original work published in 1977).

Leont'ev, A. (1994). The development of voluntary attention in the child. In R. Van der Veer & J. Valsiner (Eds.), *The Vygotsky Reader* (pp. 289–312). Oxford: Blackwell. (Original work published in 1932).

Levina, R. E. (1981). L. S. Vygotsky's ideas about the planning function of speech in children. In J. V. Wertsch (Ed.), *The concept of activity in Soviet psychology* (pp. 279–299). Armonk, NY: M. E. Sharpe.

Liaudis, V. L. (1993). Chronotypes of memory: Foundation of self-organization of the personality. *Journal of Russian and East European Psychology, 31*(4), 55–77.

Lisina, M. I. (1974). Vozrastnye i individual'nye osobennosti obschenija so vzroslymi u detej ot rozhdenija do semi let [Development and individual characteristics of communication with an adult in children from birth to age of seven]. Unpublished doctoral dissertation, Institute of General and Educational Psychology, Moscow.

Lisina, M. I., & Galiguzova, L. N. (1980). Razvitie u rebenka potrebnosti v obschenii so vzroslym i sverstnikami [The development of a child's need for communication with an adult and with peers]. In *Problemy vozrastnoj i pedagogicheskoj psikhologii.* Moscow: NIIOP APM SSSR.

Luria, A. R. (1969). Speech development and the formation of mental processes. In M. Cole & I. Maltzman (Eds.), *A handbook of contemporary Soviet psychology* (pp. 121–162). New York: Basic Books.

Luria, A. R. (1976). *Cognitive development: Its cultural and social foundations* (M. Lopez-Morillas & L. Solotaroff, Trans.). Cambridge, MA: Harvard University Press.

Luria, A. R. (1977). Speech development and the formation of mental processes. In M. Cole & I. Maltzman (Eds.), *A handbook of contemporary Soviet psychology.* New York: Basic Books. (Original work published in 1959).

Luria, A. R. (1978). Paths of development of thought in the child. In M. Cole (Ed.), *The selected writings of A. R. Luria.* White Plains, NY: M. E. Sharpe.

Luria, A. R. (1979). *The making of mind: A personal account of Soviet psychology.* (M. Cole and S. Cole, Trans.). Cambridge, MA: Harvard University Press.

Luria, A. R. (1994). The problem of the cultural behavior of the child. In R. Van der Veer & J. Valsiner (Eds.), *The Vygotsky Reader* (pp. 46–56). Oxford: Blackwell. (Original work published in 1928).

Martin, L. M. W. (1990). Detecting and defining science problems: A study of video-mediated lessons. In L. Moll (Ed.), *Vygotsky and education: Instructional implications and applications of sociohistorical psychology* (pp. 372–402). Cambridge: Cambridge University Press.

McAfee, O., & Leong, D. J. (1994). *Assessing and guiding young children's development and learning.* Boston: Allyn & Bacon.

McLeish, J. (1975). *Soviet psychology: History, theory, content.* London: Methuen.

McNeill, D. (1985). Language viewed as action. In J. Wertsch (Ed.), *Culture, communication and cognition: Vygotskian perspectives* (pp. 258–277). Cambridge: Cambridge University Press.

Meacham, J. A. (1979). The role of verbal activity in remembering the goals of actions. In G. Ziven (Ed.), *The development of self-regulation through private speech.* New York: John Wiley & Sons.

Moll, L. C., & Greenberg, J. B. (1990). Creating zones of possibilities: Combining social contexts for instruction. In L. Moll (Ed.), *Vygotsky and education: Instructional implications and applications of sociohistorical psychology* (pp. 319–348). Cambridge: Cambridge University Press.

Moll, L. C., & Whitmore, K. F. (1993). Vygotsky in classroom practice: Moving from individual transmission to social transaction. In E. A. Forman, N. Minick, & C. A. Stone (Eds.), *Contexts for learning: Sociocultural dynamics in children's development* (pp. 19–42). New York: Oxford University Press.

Mueller, E. C., & Cooper, C. R. (1986). On conceptualizing peer research. In E. C. Mueller & C. R. Cooper (Eds.), *Process and outcome in peer relationships* (pp. 3–24). Orlando, FL: Academic Press.

Musatti, T. (1986). Early peer relations: The perspectives of Piaget and Vygotsky. In E. C. Mueller & C. R. Cooper (Eds.), *Process and outcome in peer relationships* (pp. 25–50). Orlando, FL: Academic Press.

National Council of Teachers of Mathematics. (1989). *Curriculum and evaluation standards for school mathematics.* Washington, DC: Author.

Newman D., Griffin P., & Cole, M. (1989). *The construction zone: Working for cognitive change in school.* Cambridge: Cambridge University Press.

Newman F., & Holzman L. (1993). *Lev Vygotsky: Revolutionary scientist.* New York: Routledge.

Palincsar, A. S., Brown, A. L., Campione, J. C. (1993). First-grade dialogues for knowledge acquisition and use. In E. A. Forman, N. Minick, & C. A. Stone (Eds.), *Contexts for learning: Sociocultural dynamics in children's development* (pp. 43–57). New York: Oxford University Press.

Panofsky, C. P., John-Steiner, V., & Blackwell, P. J. (1990). The development of scientific concepts and discourse. In L. Moll (Ed.), *Vygotsky and education: Instructional implications and applications of sociohistorical psychology* (pp. 251–270). Cambridge: Cambridge University Press.

Paris S. G., & Winograd P. (1990). How metacognition can promote academic learning and instruction. In B. F. Jones & L. Idol (Eds.), *Dimensions of thinking and cognitive instruction.* Hillsdale, NJ: Lawrence Erlbaum.

Parke, R. D., Ornstein, P. A., Rieser, J. J., & Zahn-Waxler, C. (Eds.). (1994). *A century of developmental psychology.* Washington, DC: American Psychological Association.

Parten, M. B. (1932). Social participation among preschool children. *Journal of Abnormal and Social Psychology, 27,* 243–269.

Pedagogika Editorial Staff. (1983). L. S. Vygotsky and contemporary defectology. *Journal of Soviet Psychology, 21*(4), 79–90. (Original work published in 1982).

Perret-Clermont, A-N. (1980). *Social interaction and cognitive development in children.* New York: Academic Press.

Perret-Clermont, A-N., Perret, J-F., & Bell, N. (1991). The social construction of mean-
    ing and cognitive activity in elementary school children. In L. B. Resnick, J. M.
    Levine, & S. D. Teasley (Eds.), *Perspectives on socially shared cognition.* (pp. 41–62)
    Washington, DC: American Psychological Association.
Piaget, J. (1926). *The language and thought of the child* (M. Gabain, Trans.). London:
    Routledge & Kegan Paul. (Original work published in 1923).
Piaget, J. (1930). *The child's conception of the world* (J. Tomlinson & A. Tomlinson, Trans.).
    New York: International Universities Press. (Original work published in 1923).
Piaget, J. (1952). *The origins of intelligence in children.* New York: International Universities
    Press. (Original work published in 1936).
Piaget, J. (1962). *Play, dreams and imitation in childhood* (C. Gattegno & F. M. Hodgson,
    Trans.). New York: Norton. (Original work published in 1945).
Piaget, J., & Inhelder, B. (1969). *The psychology of the child.* New York: Basic Books.
Rahmani, L. (1973). *Soviet psychology: Philosophical, theoretical and experimental issues.* New
    York: International Universities Press.
Ratner, C. (1991). *Vygotsky's sociohistorical psychology and its contemporary applications.* New
    York: Plenum Press.
Resnick, L. B. (1991). Shared cognition: Thinking as social practice. In L. B. Resnick, J.
    M. Levine, & S. D. Teasley (Eds.), *Perspectives on socially shared cognition* (pp. 1–23)
    Washington, DC: American Psychological Association.
Roberts, R. N., & Tharp, R. G. (1980). A naturalistic study of school children's private speech
    in an academic problem-solving task. *Cognitive Therapy and Research, 4,* 341–352.
Rogoff, B. (1986). Adult assistance of children's learning. In T. E. Raphael (Ed.), *The con-
    text of school-based literacy.* New York: Random House.
Rogoff, B. (1990). *Apprenticeship in thinking: Cognitive development in social context.* New
    York: Oxford University Press.
Rogoff, B. (1991). Social interaction as apprenticeship in thinking: Guided participation
    in spatial planning. In L. B. Resnick, J. M. Levine, & S. D. Teasley (Eds.), *Perspectives
    on socially shared cognition* (pp. 349–364). Washington, DC: American Psychological
    Association.
Rogoff, B., & Lave, J. (Eds.). (1984). *Everyday cognition: Its development in social context.*
    Cambridge, MA: Harvard University Press.
Rogoff, B., Malkin, C., & Gilbride, K. (1984). Interaction with babies as guidance in de-
    velopment. *New Directions for Child Development, 23,* 31–44.
Rogoff, B., Mistry, J. Goncu, A., & Mosier, C. (1993). Guided participation in cultural ac-
    tivity by toddlers and caregivers. *Monographs of the Society for Research in Child
    Development, 58*(8), Serial No. 236.
Rogoff, B., Mosier, C., Mistry, J., & Goncu, A. (1993). Toddlers' guided participation with
    their caregivers in cultural activity. In E. A. Forman, N. Minick, & C. A. Stone
    (Eds.), *Contexts for learning: Sociocultural dynamics in children's development* (pp.
    230–253). New York: Oxford University Press.
Rommetveit, R. (1985). Language acquisition as increasing linguistic structuring of experi-
    ence and symbolic behavior control. In J. Wertsch (Ed.), *Culture, communication and cog-
    nition: Vygotskian perspectives* (pp. 183–204). Cambridge: Cambridge University Press.
Rubin, K. H. (1979). The impact of the natural setting on private speech. In G. Ziven
    (Ed.), *The development of self-regulation through private speech* (pp. 265–294). New
    York: John Wiley & Sons.
Rubin, K. H. (1980). Fantasy play: Its role in the development of social skills and social cog-
    nition. In K. H. Rubin (Ed.), *Children's play* (pp. 69–84). San Francisco: Jossey-Bass.

Rubtsov, V. V. (1981). The role of cooperation in the development of intelligence. *Soviet Psychology, 23*, 65–84.

Rubtsov, V. V. (1991). *Learning in children: Organization and development of cooperative actions.* New York: Nova Science Publishers.

Ruzskaya, A. G., Elagina, M. G., & Zalysina, I. A. (1989). The development of speech among children in communication with adults during the first seven years. *Journal of Soviet Psychology, 27*(5), 54–67. (Original work published in 1986).

Sakharov, L. (1994). Methods for investigating concepts. In R. Van der Veer & J. Valsiner (Eds.), *The Vygotsky Reader* (pp. 46–56). Oxford: Blackwell. (Original work published in 1930).

Sapir, E. (1921). *Language: An introduction to the study of speech.* New York: Harcourt Brace.

Saxe, G. B., Gearhart, M., & Guberman, S. R. (1984). The social organization of early number development. *New Directions for Child Development, 23,* 19–30.

Schickendanz, J. A. (1982). The acquisition of written language in young children. In B. Spodek (Ed.), *Handbook of research in early childhood education,* (pp. 242–263). New York: Free Press.

Scribner, S. (1977). Modes of thinking and ways of speaking: Culture and logic reconsidered. In P. N. Johnson-Laird & P. S. Wason (Eds.), *Thinking: Readings in cognitive science* (pp. 483–500). Cambridge: Cambridge University Press.

Shotter, J. (1989). Vygotsky's psychology: Joint activity in a developmental zone. *New Ideas in Psychology, 7*(2), 185–207.

Slavin, R. (1994). *Practical guide to cooperative learning.* Boston: Allyn & Bacon.

Slobin, D. I. (Ed.). (1966). *Handbook of Soviet psychology.* White Plains, NY: International Arts and Sciences Press.

Sloutsky, V. (1991). Sravnenie faktornoj struktury intellekta u semejnych detej i vospitannikov detskogo doma [Comparison of factor structure of intelligence among family-reared and orphanage-reared children]. *Vestnik Moskovskogo Universiteta, 1,* 34–41.

Smilansky, S., & Shefatya, L. (1990). *Facilitating play: A medium for promoting cognitive, socio-emotional, and academic development in young children.* Gaithersburg, MD: Psychosocial and Educational Publications.

Smolucha, F. (1992). Social origins of private speech in pretend play. In R. M. Diaz & L. E. Berk (Eds.), *Private speech: From social interaction to self-regulation* (pp. 123–141). Cambridge: Cambridge University Press.

Solomon, G. (Ed.). (1993). *Distributed cognitions: Psychological and educational considerations.* Cambridge: Cambridge University Press.

Spector, J. E. (1992). Predicting progress in beginning reading: Dynamic assessment of phonemic awareness. *Journal of Educational Psychology, 84*(3), 353–363.

Spitz, R. A. (1946). Anaclitic depression. *Psychoanalytic Study of the Child, 2,* 313–342.

Stone, C. A. (1993). What is missing in the metaphor of scaffolding? In E. A. Forman, N. Minick, & C. A. Stone (Eds.), *Contexts for learning: Sociocultural dynamics in children's development* (pp. 169–183). New York: Oxford University Press.

Stroufe, L. A. (1983). Infant-caregiver attachment and patterns of adaptation in preschool: The roots of maladaptation and competence. In M. Perlmutter (Ed.), *Minnesota symposium in child psychology* (Vol. 16, pp. 41–81). Hillsdale, NJ: Erlbaum.

Sutherland, P. (1992). *Cognitive development today: Piaget and his critics.* London: Paul Chapman.

Teale, W. H. & Sulzby, E. (Eds.). (1986) *Emergent literacy: Writing and reading.* Norwood, NJ: Ablex.

Telesina, T. L., & Pisareva, M. L. (1992). Correlation between the level of development of intellectual actions and emotions: Experiences of preschoolers in a play situation. *Journal of Russian and East European Psychology, 30*(4), 45–56.

Tharp, R. G., & Gallimore, R. (1988). *Rousing minds to life: Teaching, learning and schooling in social context.* Cambridge: Cambridge University Press.

Tronick, E. Z. (1989). Emotions and emotional communication in infants. *American Psychologist, 44,* 115–123.

Tudge, J. (1990). Vygotsky, the zone of proximal development, and peer collaboration: Implications for classroom practice. In L. Moll (Ed.), *Vygotsky and education: Instructional implications and applications of sociohistorical psychology* (pp. 155–176). Cambridge: Cambridge University Press.

Tudge, J. (1992). Processes and consequences of peer collaboration: A Vygotskian analysis. *Child Development, 63,* 1364–1379.

Valsiner, J. (1984). Construction of the zone of proximal development in adult-child joint action: The socialization of means. *New Directions for Child Development, 23,* 65–76.

Valsiner, J. (1988). *Developmental psychology in the Soviet Union.* Bloomington: Indiana University Press.

Valsiner, J. (1989). *Human development and culture: The social nature of personality and its study.* Lexington, MA: Lexington Books.

Van der Veer, R., & Valsiner, J. (1991). *Understanding Vygotsky: A quest for synthesis.* Oxford: Blackwell.

Venger, A. L., & Polivanova, K. N. (1990). Distinctive features of 6 year olds in relation to adult-assigned tasks. *Soviet Psychology, 28*(5) 42–53.

Venger, L. A. (1977). The emergence of perceptual actions. In M. Cole (Ed.), *Soviet developmental psychology: An anthology.* White Plains, NY: Sharpe. (Original work published in 1969).

Venger, L. A. (Ed.) (1986). *Razvitije poznavatel'nych sposobnostey v protsesse doshkol'nogo vospitanija* [Development of cognitive abilities through preschool education]. Moscow: Pedagogika.

Venger, L. A. (1988). The origin and development of cognitive abilities in preschool children. *International Journal of Behavioral Development, 11*(2), 147–153.

Vocate, D. R. (1987). *The theory of A. R. Luria: Functions of spoken language in the development of higher mental processes.* Hillsdale, NJ: Lawrence Erlbaum.

Vygotsky, L. S. (1962). *Thought and language* (E. Hanfmann and G. Vokar, Trans.). Cambridge MA: MIT Press. (Original work published in 1934).

Vygotsky, L. S. (1971). *The psychology of art.* Cambridge MA: MIT Press. (Original work published in 1968).

Vygotsky, L. S. (1977). Play and its role in the mental development of the child. In M. Cole (Ed.), *Soviet developmental psychology* (pp. 76–99). White Plains, NY: M. E. Sharpe. (Original work published in 1966).

Vygotsky, L. S. (1978). *Mind and society: The development of higher mental processes.* Cambridge, MA: Harvard University Press. (Original work published in 1930, 1933, 1935).

Vygotsky, L. S. (1983). *Sobranie sochinenii: Tom tretij Problemy razvitiya psikhiki* [Collected works: Vol. 3. Problems of mental development]. Moscow: Izdatel'stvo Pedagogika.

Vygotsky, L. S. (1984). *Sobranie sochinenii: Tom chetvertyj. Detskaya psikhologiya* [Collected works: Vol 4. Child psychology]. Moscow: Izdatel'stvo Pedagogika.

Vygotsky, L. S. (1987). *The collected works of L. S. Vygotsky* (R. W. Rieber & A. S. Carton, Trans.). New York: Plenum Press. (Original works published in 1934, 1960).

Vygotsky, L. S. (1993). *The collected works of L. S. Vygotsky* (Vols. 1–2). New York: Plenum Press. (Original work published in 1920–1930).

Vygotsky, L. S. (1994a). The problem of the environment. In R. Van der Veer & J. Valsiner (Eds.), *The Vygotsky Reader* (pp. 338–354). Oxford: Blackwell. (Original work published in 1935).

Vygotsky, L. S. (1994b). The development of academic concepts in school-aged children. In R. van der Veer & J. Valsiner (Eds.), *The Vygotsky Reader* (pp. 355–370). Oxford: Blackwell. (Original work published in 1935).

Vygotsky, L. S., & Luria, A. R. (1993) *Studies in the history of behavior: Ape, primitive, and child.* Hillsdale, NJ: Lawrence Erlbaum. (Original work published in 1930).

Vygotsky, L. S., & Luria, A. (1994). Tool and symbol in child development. In R. Van der Veer & J. Valsiner (Eds.), *The Vygotsky Reader* (pp. 99–174). Oxford: Blackwell. (Original work published in 1984).

Watson, J. B. (1970). *Behaviorism* (rev. ed.). New York: Norton. (Original work published in 1924).

Wells, G. (Ed.). (1981). *Learning through interaction: The study of language development* (Vol. 1). Cambridge: Cambridge University Press.

Wertsch, J. V. (1979). The regulation of human action and the give-new organization of private speech. In G. Zivin (Ed.), *The development of self-regulation through private speech* (pp. 79–98). New York: John Wiley & Sons.

Wertsch, J. V. (1980). The significance of dialogue in Vygotsky's account of social, ego-centric, and inner speech. *Contemporary Educational Psychology, 22,* 1–22.

Wertsch, J. V. (1985a). *Vygotsky and the social formation of mind.* Cambridge, MA: Harvard University Press.

Wertsch, J. V. (Ed.). (1985b). *Culture communication and cognition: Vygotskian perspectives.* Cambridge: Cambridge University Press.

Wertsch, J. V. (1991a). *Voices of the mind: A sociocultural approach to mediated action.* Cambridge, MA: Harvard University Press.

Wertsch, J. V. (1991b). A sociocultural approach to socially shared cognition. In L. B. Resnick, J. M. Levine, & S. D. Teasley (Eds.), *Perspectives on socially shared cognition.* (pp. 85–100). Washington, DC: American Psychological Association.

Wertsch, J. V., & Tulviste, P. (1994). Lev Semynovich Vygotsky and contemporary developmental psychology. In R. D. Parke, P. A. Ornstein, J. J. Reiser, & C. Zahn-Waxler (Eds.), *A century of developmental psychology* (pp. 333–356). Washington, DC: American Psychological Association.

Whorf, B. L. (1956). Science and linguistics. In J. B. Carrol (Ed.), *Language, thought and reality: Selected writings of Benjamin Lee Whorf* (pp. 207–219). Cambridge, MA: MIT Press.

Wilson, J. W. (Ed.). (1975). *Analyses of reasoning processes.* Chicago: University of Chicago.

Wood, D., Bruner, J. C., & Ross, G. (1976). The role of tutoring in problem solving. *Journal of Child Psychology and Psychiatry, 17,* 89–100.

Zaporozhets, A. V. (1970). The development of perception in the preschool child. In *Cognitive development in children* (pp. 647–665). Chicago, IL: University of Chicago Press.

Zaporozhets, A. V. (1977). Some of the psychological problems of sensory training in early childhood and the preschool period. In M. Cole & I. Maltzman (Eds.), *A handbook of contemporary Soviet psychology.* New York: Basic Books. (Original published in 1959).

Zaporozhets, A. (1986). *Izbrannye psickologicheskie trudy* [Selected works]. Moscow: Pedagogika.

Zaporozhets, A. V., & Lukov, U. D. (1979). The development of reasoning in young children. *Soviet Psychology, 18*(2), 47–66.

Zaporozhets, A. V., & Markova, T. A. (1983). Principles of preschool pedagogy: Part 1. *Soviet Education, 25,* 8–11.

Zinchenko, V. P. (1985). Vygotsky's ideas about units for the analysis of mind. In J. V. Wertsch (Ed.), *Culture, communication and cognition: Vygotskian perspectives* (pp. 94–118). Cambridge: Cambridge University Press.

Zivin, G. (Ed.). (1979). *The development of self-regulation through private speech.* New York: John Wiley & Sons.

Zukow-Goldring, P., & Ferko, K. R. (1994). An ecological approach to the emergence of lexicon: Socializing attention. In V. John-Steiner, C. P. Panofsky, & L. W. Smith (Eds.), *Sociocultural approaches to language and literacy: An interactionist perspective.* Cambridge: Cambridge University Press.

Author Index

Subject Index